01209 721302
http://webopac.cornwall.ac.uk
rosewarne.learningcentre@duchy.ac.uk

THE Learning CENTRE

Duchy College Rosewarne
Learning Centre

l
h
w
V
th
an
an

...angie.com

The Polair Self-Help Series

IN A NEW LIGHT *Anna Hayward*
THE MEDITATION LIFESTYLE *Colum Hayward*
NOW WE'RE COPING *Chris Sangster*

NOW WE'RE COPING

HOLISTIC STRATEGIES FOR DIFFICULT TIMES

Chris Sangster

Polair
Publishing

POLAIR PUBLISHING
LONDON
www.polairpublishing.co.uk

First published 2013

British Library Cataloguing-in-Publication Data
A catalogue record for this book is available from the
British Library

ISBN 978-1-905398-30-0

Cover design:
Guilherme Gustavo Condeixa

Set in 11.5 on 14 pt Joanna at the Publisher and Printed in
Great Britain by Halstan & Co., Amersham, Bucks.

CONTENTS

FOREWORD

THIS BOOK initially evolved during an interesting hospitalization experience. As I lay there, experiencing new traumas and interventions on a daily basis, my mind kept comparing my trials with the problems I had experienced over the years with stinging nettles, the plant on the cover of this book, while living in the countryside in Scotland and England. I'll describe the biology of how they irritate the skin in greater detail later – but as I recalled the pain they produce, I realized in that hospital bed that one could combat the nasty effects of that stinging plant if you grasped it positively, rather than letting it aggravate your skin by brushing against it.

Not all countries have the stinging nettle as such – but I guess all countries have their own equivalent of some annoying plants that causes irritating rashes. And thence, we probably all experience 'life's nettles' in some form, as irritants, problems and upsets.

As a management training consultant for many years, I had been involved in applying business practices – often referred to as 'best practice'. In latter years, as I became more interested and involved in 'matters spiritual', I came to modify and adapt many of these ideas to apply in the 'broader church' of life generally. These techniques incorporated the likes of meditation with stress management and sounding with communication.

While in hospital, with time on my hands during an extended treatment regime, I had the opportunity to develop these more generally-applicable stress-management and mind-focus techniques to become valuable as a coping strategy. Impressed by the success of the strategy born through focusing on the Now, the content of this book began to grow in my mind.

Based on a detailed examination of a wide range of practical examples and experiences, gained during a varied life in a range of locations, my hospital experiences, experience of writing several other books and the aforementioned experience in business consultancy, this book provides food for thought for you, the reader, to establish your own preferred strategies. I prefer to write primarily from my own experiences, reading and discussions with others, as this allows me to elaborate more deeply on the implications and conclusions. These examples, as well as periodic exercises, are designed to provide you with further food for thought.

One of my developing interests has been the application of spirituality in the workplace – where we have a heightened level of awareness and mindfulness towards there being something 'extra', which can be applied in a more altruistic way of thinking in day-to-day, as well as business affairs. This spirituality doesn't directly stem from particular religions or beliefs – it is purely a way of thinking clearly and unselfishly, reaching decisions which best satisfy the common good. Through examples and elaboration, this theme will evolve further as the chapters progress.

The theme throughout is thinking about and applying coping strategies, when things are less than perfect. Additionally, when we're considering some of the areas of business 'best practice', the angle is slightly different. Here, we will be considering 'work' methods and techniques which can be applied in our normal life, to reduce or prevent some of the situations which could otherwise cause us stress. Thus, we're looking at the possibilities of prevention rather than cure – but the activities can still be considered as coping strategies.

There is no single, correct answer; there is no single path down which you are being directed. There is however a range of possible suggestions, honestly and lovingly presented – a range which you, the reader, may wish to consider when developing your own coping strategies, in gently grasping and embracing the identified nettles of your own life. Consider, adapt and apply – the answer to a less stressful and more positive life is certainly within your grasp.

I should like to thank the many wonderful people who have shone their light on me and helped me grow in stature and understanding. I would particularly like to mention Yeva and Isabelle, Kathryn, my late wife Gillean and my partner Jackie for all the support, listening and discussion they have provided for me – and continue to provide from the present life and beyond. I would also like to thank Colum Hayward, my publisher, for believing in the message I had to impart and for coping admirably and patiently with the various refinement nettles we ploughed our way through along the way! My thanks to the White Eagle Publishing Trust for permission to use extracts from White Eagle's teaching.

The path towards empowerment and enlightenment is long and convoluted, and we all need as much help and support as possible to help us along the way. I hope that this book gives you some of that illuminated support – and that your future journey is as fascinating and expansive as mine has already been!

Chris Sangster
Liss, Hampshire, England : April 2013
www.the-integrated-triangle.com

CHAPTER ONE

LIFE'S NETTLES,
AND COPING WITH THEM

I'M IMAGINING that one reason why you're reading this may be that you've gone through a few crises in your life. Yes, so have I. I guess most of us have, one way or another.

There's a whole range of these 'one way or another' crisis situations. There's the medical crisis, the job crisis, the financial crisis, the family crisis, the bereavement crisis, the interpersonal crisis (a fancy way of saying you've fallen out with someone big time!), legal problems or an infrastructure crisis (your home flooding or a tree falling through your roof, for example). There are probably many more as well, because we're all just a little bit different and unique. Under each heading, there's also an absolute legion of possible events. We can't begin to cover them all here as, to some extent, each will be unique to the person or people experiencing it – that's YOU as well as others.

What we can do, however, is look at a range of strategies to apply, in order to cope when they come and to be ready for some of the next crisis-nettles that threaten to sting us as we journey through life. Then, by thinking these through in the light of your own unique experiences, you'll be able to apply and adapt them to come up with your own personal strategies, to apply when the moment arrives. This is both focused self-help and positive forward planning – looking to the future, in order to prepare yourselves mentally. By doing this, you will be ready with some possible strategies which you can adapt and apply when that next new crisis threatens. We'll also be able to consider some 'best practice' strategies, which may reduce the number of future situations which cause these crises in the first place.

Reviewing those Options

Thinking into the future to establish possible strategies is a truly positive action, identifying both structured and creative responses. It's using both left and right parts of the brain. It's being constructive. And, it makes it easier to meet and cope with problems positively, when the need arises. Which it inevitably will, from time to time.

There is an opposite. Some years ago, there was a saying which was popular with both a large multiple store and the UK government of the time – 'There is no "Plan B"'. This was trumpeted endlessly, in the belief that it depicted decisive leadership. When, totally predictably, 'Plan A' began to hit the fan, it created the opposite image, of the leadership failing to achieve their single, unique goal. Having a 'Plan B' – and indeed a 'Plan C' and onwards – helps us cope with change and eases the decision-making process to allow potential revision of our plans, so as to maintain progress.

Future Thinking

There can be a subtle difference here, which it's very important to underline at this time, when thinking in terms of past, present and future.

The more negative way of thinking into the future, looking for problems, is not what this book's about. We do encounter it quite a lot, however. It's tinged with the elements of fear and stress. It's the 'what could go wrong if....' type of thinking. This is less helpful for our crisis-coping preparations. Let's consider a simple example.

Example: Walking Barefoot

Imagine you're walking along a path, barefoot. The sun is shining and the birds are singing – and you can hear them because you don't have any of today's world-eliminating earphones wedged into your ears! Life is good – until suddenly you stand on a rusty nail sticking out of piece of wood. You collapse to the ground, holding your foot … perhaps even hollering a little. Then your mind kicks in. Will I get gangrene? When did I last have a tetanus jab? What happens if the bleeding doesn't stop? Will I be able to walk back to civilization? The fear of things going wrong and the possible bad outcomes from your action hangs like an ever-darkening shadow over you.

What happens if the same thing happens to a dog? It yelps a little, perhaps, licks the hurt paw and limps on down the track – with the limp gradually decreasing. If a cat happened to cross its path at this point, the dog would be racing off after it, totally forgetting about its recent injury. The dog exists in the Now. It doesn't have any real concept of the future, other than as a sequence of 'Now' moments running one after the other. Standing on the nail was one 'Now' moment; chasing the cat was another, separate 'Now' moment.

Future and Past

We can learn from the animals and try to live more in the present – in the Now. Worrying less about what could go wrong in the future will relieve those stressful, fearful attitudes. We'll be concentrating a lot on this idea of focusing on the Now, as we progress in this book through our range of crises and ways of coping with them. Really focusing on the Now – only on the present moment – is a way of eliminating as many of the negative issues as possible. We'll be reviewing this and how dwelling on past, as well as future worries, can accentuate our coping problems. Focusing solely on the Now can take us to a higher level, where nothing – *nothing* – else matters at that moment.

It's strange the way many people dwell on their negative past experiences, as opposed to constructive and positive memories. Asking a variety of people the simple question – 'how was your holiday?' I would bet that, after two or three opening sentences, the majority of them are giving you instances of the bad weather, tummy bug, overpriced restaurants, the pick-pocketing incident, and so on. Like newspaper reporting, they tend to focus automatically on the negative things that have gone before, forgetting to mention the good things in life.

Keeping a Perspective on Life

So, that's something to keep reminding yourself. You may be currently having a crisis. You might have just come out of another. They might even have run more or less on top of one another – but there will be the better things to focus on, to lift you up off the ground between those potentially negative experiences – and subsequently. And there will be good elements, even amid the crisis, bringing happy experiences upon which memories are built.

Example: Caring for Mother-in-Law

My late wife Gillean and I cared for her mother in her final months after she had an inoperable brain tumour diagnosed. 'M-in-L', as I called her (short for Mother-in-Law, obviously!) was an amazing woman – when this problem surfaced, they discovered she'd no medical records to speak of, as prior to this she'd never officially been ill! After retirement, she'd taken up embroidery and quiltmaking in a big way – she was a very creative woman, with positive views of what she believed in (and didn't believe in!). As her brain deteriorated, she became more childlike and dependent – latterly, I had to tap each of her thighs in turn while supporting her, to remind her to move her legs – but we had some memorable and close times together, in those final weeks. Gillean, understandably, had a frustrated anger that her mother was slipping away so fast, in a state which was alien to her but I was happy to be able to assist M-in-L (her real name was Hilary but it seemed disrespectful to call her that!) in a way I hadn't managed to do during the final months of my own mother, who died more impersonally, in hospital. Perhaps that was part of my positive feelings, as I was being allowed to personally make amends to some extent. There are invariably some lovely wildflowers amongst the nettles, if you look – so take advantage of their presence, when you can!

Considering each Moment

When looking at past, present and future, there are potentially both positive and negative responses. Note – they're
not 'good' and 'bad'. Think of any current or potential pre-
dicament as being the same as a battery, where both positive
and negative are required to make the energy flow. As with
the passage of energy in the battery, the positive produces
the dynamic, while the negative provides the grounding, or
earth. Life is like that too.

The past thus gives us experience, which can be brought
to the table to help to refine and improve new initiatives.

Awareness of these past experiences can also assist in the
positive side of planning future responses. This awareness
makes it easier to implement change, when things don't go
according to that initially-considered 'Plan A'. As I identified
earlier, however, future thinking should not encourage fearful or stressful imaginings of what might be – or, more to
the point, what might go wrong.

Crisis Situations

When analysing a crisis, we're looking for positively and
objectively thought-through reactions and responses. What
do we mean by 'objectively'? It means we're considering
things logically, with a focus on the expected, or even
intended, end-result. The mere act of thinking through
these steps and stages towards a possible future resolution
will help us identify the causes and effects of the crisis – and
highlight some of the key problem areas. Being more aware
of these – and giving ourselves the luxury of time to consider

possible options – will help us cope more comfortably with the crisis. This, in turn, will allow us to be in a state where we're thinking logically – and not panicking.

Separating the Source from the Concerns

We'll consider this idea in greater detail slightly later but it's important to establish the principle at this point. Think about this equation for a moment:

$$CRISIS = SOURCE + CONCERNS$$

For any given crisis, there will be a source (cancer, a death, a major accident, a large debt, etc.) which will cause us to have concerns (worry, panic, fear, sleeplessness, and so on). It's very important first to subdivide these two elements, before trying to address them.

Many of the strategies we'll be considering will be primarily addressing the concerns you have. We can hopefully do something about alleviating these. Of course, many of your concerns are likely to be relating to how you can respond to the source. But at least you've first gone through the process of identifying what the key source of the crisis is.

You're less likely to be able to address these major source-problems on your own and, generalizing slightly, you'll usually need some type of professional input, such as your GP, a hospital specialist, financial adviser, lawyer, structural engineer or surveyor.

Having access to whatever professional specialist(s) are appropriate for your crisis will give you some degree of support. Their inputs may not eliminate the problem totally but will leave you feeling at least that a) you're not alone and b) most of what can be done to address the source is being done. It may take time but it's progressing!

Facing up to the source makes it more possible for you to concentrate on your various concerns – and the strategies you can apply for coping more confidently with them.

Exercise: it's 'Review a Crisis' Time!

So, pause for a moment here. Take time to identify a crisis that you've personally experienced in the fairly recent past. We listed suggestions of some key areas at the beginning of the chapter. Perhaps you can think of one that went a bit 'pear-shaped' – that didn't resolve in the way you would have liked.

As a first stage, try to identify what you would consider to be the source of the crisis. This might need a bit of de-tailed consideration – and honesty! Once you've focused on the source, you can then proceed towards isolating some of your key concerns.

With the luxury (if that's the correct word!) of being able to review what happened slowly and dispassionately, you should be able to reopen the past more positively. We haven't considered a range of strategies yet for doing so – these come in chapter three – but give some thought to the real blockages which got in your way, which gradu-ally created the source problem. Blockages can mean lots of things – people, lack of resources or finances, attitudes, beliefs (yours and others'), regulations, conditions, genera-tion-differences … the list can go on and on.

Now, think in the present or Now. Think about the key source problem again – and the concerns which spiralled over time. If you were re-running your 'film' of the situation with the benefit of hindsight, what might you do differently this time? How could you respond helpfully to some of these key blockages in a more positive way? Could you cause some of them to become more positive – or at least more flexible? Are there ways of bypassing some of the more intransigent ones?

Now, consider for a moment whether some of your concerns might have been smaller and/or more manageable, if you'd been more in control of how the source problem was unfolding. Perhaps you might agree that being able to focus more objectively on the source will be helpful in coping with some of these concerns.

Notice – we're using a review of past activities and decisions positively here, in order to react differently in the Now, or present. We're not worrying unduly about future possibilities which might cloud our revised plans – although we're obviously conscious of the potential, because we're reviewing past experiences in order to re-decide our present strategy. That is positively focusing on the Now.

OK – so have you given that selected crisis some considered thought? Or are you just reading on, regardless? There will be a variety of opportunities to pause for specific reflections during your reading of this book. Please give yourself the time for these reflective moments! You'll reap the benefits later.

So, having got your head round the flexible way of thinking that we need to apply (I hope), spend a few moments thinking through your identified crisis – that particular nettle which you had to grasp or embrace – reviewing what you might do next time round, when a similar situation appears on your path through life.

Living for the Moment

Some of us will have experienced a crisis which may have influenced our life, after it was resolved. Because of advances in medical science, for example, there are many relatively young people who though their lives have been saved are now living their current existence as single or multiple amputees. I find it hard to even begin to understand the changes which that situation must bring to living in their particular Now. However, one of the wonderful things which came from the increased emphasis and involvement of the 2012 Paralympic Games was the blossoming of disabled human participation and achievement in sport, which was a real lesson to many. One of the rash of stories which came from the widespread public exposure was that of the young child who, looking at a picture of pirate Long John Silver with his hand/hook and wooden leg, identified him as a strangely-dressed athlete!

Like changed physical capabilities, financial circumstances can also alter. Every time there is a major hurricane in America, say, we experience TV images of uninsured former homeowners standing outside the total devastation which had been their family residence the day before – and talking positively about how thankful they are to be alive – and about rebuilding their life once more.

Meditative Thought

Whatever our own crisis may be, we will be aware of the experiences of others – and how the human spirit can rise above these adversities. Where appropriate, I will include one of my poems to illustrate the awareness behind each chapter.

When I was around ten and living in Scotland, I remember a tramp coming to our door, asking for food and water. Those many years later, I can still picture this tranquil and peaceful man, who had undoubtedly experienced some major crisis to create a situation in which he was permanently walking the countryside. He was a truly gentle man and memories of him encouraged the poem that follows.

The Gentleman of the Road

He appears, approaching in the distance:
Bowed figure, walks with measured pace,
With steady tread, plods in boots long fractured,
Great-coat collar. Shroud protects his face.

What tales are captured in that figure?
What acts portrayed in walnut hands?
No recent reject from an urban marriage
Nor fallen soldier, late from Afghan sands.

Many years have seen him cross the country
Moving on he knows not why or where.
Many barns have heard his peaceful snoring,
Many dawns have lit his dew-capped hair.

Coming closer, now we see his profile:
Beard combed proudly, long hair loosely back,
Peaceful smile that says 'I have no mortgage',
Contents of his life in rope-tied sack.

Pace perks up, as if he wants to show us,
Stepping tall – but always without haste

Like a monk, he counts on acts of kindness
Meeting needs, without the call for waste.

Passing greeting, eyes in silent contact,
Head inclines, with measured deference slight,
Tin held out, to ask for drink of water;
Hunk of bread – providing meal tonight.

Speech so quiet, accent born from ancients,
Tells us tales, results of spiritual acts,
Gentle face, skin leathered by the climate,
Easy gestures, emphasize the facts.

Hand to brow, enacting old retainer
Must move on now; time cannot stand still,
Though open schedule, old limbs must keep
      moving
With final nod, our new friend breasts the hill.

Oh we, who work and live consumption,
Learn, from simple life portrayed
How, through pressures of society
From root requirements, our life-paths have
      strayed.

Link with nature, live a life holistic –
Grasp the moment, meet our basic needs.
Live and love, respect those differing values,
Learn from others, bless the life we lead.

                                        Chris Sangster

CHAPTER TWO

LIVING IN THE NOW

FAIRLY RECENTLY, as I've mentioned, I found myself hospitalized for almost a month, with a developing range of treatments and surgery. Some large part of the process that I brought into play for dealing with these hospital procedures involved focusing on the Now. We will consider this and other coping strategies in detail in the next chapter. I don't have any empirical scientific proof but, from direct observation and experience, I have a theory that some appreciable element of the pain we experience comes through the fact that we imagine the possible outcomes and results. Remember the previous example regarding the rusty nail. We imagine all the potentially dire outcomes – and suffer accordingly. Animals live in the Now, so the moment passes rapidly – and usually with few longterm ill-effects.

There are many documented examples of indigenous individuals (Australian aborigines and native American Indians, for example) who have 'self-healed' very rapidly, even from fractured bones, because of their greater ability to believe in the power of Now. By focusing on this, they can bring in healing energy very powerfully, in ways that our cultures can barely now remember. For me, really shutting down my mind from all the 'ifs' and 'buts', focusing on the Now moment rather than the procedure, helped me to cope to a greater degree, in those potentially difficult times.

Walking Mindfully

I used to go out walking late at night with my dog, Star. When it had been raining and the pavements were wet, slugs and snails came out in droves under the cover of darkness. I hate the sound of crunching snail shells under foot so, as I walked, I had to be very mindful of where I placed my feet. This is concentration on the present ... an example of being mindfully in the Now. In similar vein, when you stop everything to take in – *really* take in – a beautiful sunset, a starlit sky, a butterfly settled on a vibrant flower, a 'mindful revelation' or maybe a piece of music or artwork that really brings a lump to your throat – these are all Now moments, where you are totally focused on that particular experience.

Two More Animal-based Examples

In Scotland, I had a flock of around a hundred and fifty sheep on my land, including my own purebred Scottish blackface sheep, so have made something of a study of the ways of sheep. Shepherds will tell you that sheep have a 'death wish'. If they get caught in a thicket of brambles or blackberries, they will not struggle but will just stand still, often until they ultimately die. They are in the Now at each moment and cannot foresee the future, to understand the possible direness of their situation. If however, a human or dog comes up close, that then becomes a threat which must (in the Now) be responded to, so the sheep will struggle, break free from the thicket and run off. It doesn't make the sheep stupid or brainless – it merely cannot foresee the outcome of future actions. It lives in the Now. Incidentally, look out for that while out walking – you could save a sheep's life!

Dogs (and young babies for that matter), have no concept of 'in five minutes'. If a baby wants milk and there is none to hand, it will immediately cry. If I were to use the magic word 'walkies' with Star, she would immediately look enthusiastic. If I then went off to check for final emails, she would move away and lie down again. The 'Now' moment had passed without the activity associated with going for a walk happening – so in her mind, it was obviously a false promise. However, she would still remain alert if I went to the toilet (having got used to the strange concept of humans going to the toilet before going out for a walk designed to allow the dog to go!) and also while I put on my walking shoes, as these actions linked with her chain of 'Now' moments moving forward.

Coping in the 'Now' Moment

Prior to each hospital procedure, I brought myself to the point of being totally in that moment. I didn't think about what might happen; what might go wrong. This involved focusing deeply on the inner body, before fearful thoughts of future potential implications could kick in. At those particular 'Now' moments, I was thinking about nothing else – absolutely nothing else mattered. The same technique can be applied for tackling any potentially unwelcome undertaking, as we'll consider slightly later.

We have to cope with many activities throughout our lives which we would rather not do – but which we carry out anyway. Before parenthood (or adult caring), the thought of wiping a baby's dirty bottom or mopping up someone's sickness would perhaps fill us with revulsion. When the moment arrives, we do it, almost without a second thought. Some of us have spent years travelling to work in crowded trains and buses, with our first experiences each day being packed together in a potentially insanitary and uncomfortable manner. We do it, as it is a necessary part of the employment process in busier urban areas — but cope with it by shutting off from the world around us, using music, newspaper reading or focusing within, through contemplation or even meditation.

Mindfulness

There is an increased interest today in the concept of mindfulness — of living in and focusing on the moment. It is something that has happened during meditation since the start of time, getting to a level of focus where external distractions can be blocked out dramatically.

Think of a moment. Think of this moment, as you're reading this next sentence.

You have the luxury of having the time to read this sentence. You can think about the meaning, as it impacts on you. You can be conscious of the sounds and life around you, at that point in time. You do not think about how the experience might influence something which has happened to you in the past. You do not think about the results spinning off into the future, influenced by the current activity.

You are mindful only of the moment. In fact, you are now a paragraph further on in your appreciation of the Now existence — so you are in fact now mindful of a fresh moment in time … and have begun to defocus on what happened in the previous moment. And so, life moves on.

This is (as a 'physical' consideration) the 'Now' moment, as it sits between past and future – a concentration on what is currently happening, without potentially stress-making distractions. As we delve more deeply into mindfulness, through mental relaxation and meditative practice, we can reach a deeper Now moment, in the sense of being completely in (or within) the moment. This takes time to achieve, of course – the moment when we can 'go within' to feel and experience with both mind and heart – so in the final chapter we will return to some of the thought-processes involved. This will allow time for the necessary awareness to progress a little further!

Buddhist monks practise mindful walking – measured walking on a prescribed path – to encourage focused contemplation. You too can walk – and even sit – mindfully. It doesn't really require skill – it only requires focus, good intention and concentration.

Focus on the Moment

One of the problems that occurred during my stay in hospital was that the past began to blur. I was being regularly asked to provide detail of procedures which had happened in the past days and weeks – and it became increasingly hard to do this. Even in writing this book at the manuscript stage, as the weeks and months pass from the time of my discharge, the detail becomes increasingly forgotten.

We can perhaps consider this as an act of 'blotting out' the unwelcome past. Ask any woman who has gone through the pain, trials and tribulations of childbirth and who then consciously opts to repeat the process! As one tends to think more in the 'Now' moment, the need to actually remember past detail potentially diminishes. Experience is, of course, valuable and potentially applicable – often, preconceived fears are not.

Relate while you Can

One obvious benefit of focusing on the Now is that we tend not to retain past grudges against others, as we are no longer dwelling on the past. In recent months, I have come across several families whose members have not spoken to each other for months or years because of some perceived slight in the past. In one particular case, there was some attempt at reconciliation shortly before the death of one member, through cancer. I would place money on the possibility that the remaining member experiences regrets at not speaking more while she could. There is a saying in my inspirational book MESSAGES FROM THE MOUNTAINS: 'Talk while you can – death ends the conversation'. Any of us who have experienced close bereavement will doubtless have experienced the moment after the loved one's death where one simply wanted to turn to that person and say something or share a thought or action. Too late! If you have meaningful thoughts to impart, Now is the time to speak.

Looking to the Future

Notice, I'm not suggesting that we should use thinking in the Now as a reason for shimmying through life without any forward thought or planning. I'm thinking here more about the 'if only' type of forward thinking – the display of disinterest or disdain in what is currently happening, borne on the belief that we will move on to something better in the future. It often won't be any better – but the net result is that the possible range of benefits from the present activity and the sense of value in it have been potentially lost.

Concentrating on the Now

In his book, THE POWER OF NOW, Eckhart Tolle differentiates between what he calls 'clock time' and 'psychological time', as two elements supplementing his all-important focus on the Now. He states, 'Learn to use time in the practical aspects of your life – we may call this "clock time" – but immediately return to present-moment awareness when those practical matters have been dealt with.'

Slightly later, he continues, 'If you set yourself a goal and work toward it, you are using clock time. You are aware of where you want to go, but you honour and give your fullest attention to the step that you are taking at the moment. If you then become excessively focused on the goal, perhaps because you are seeking happiness, fulfilment, or a more complete sense of self in it, the Now is no longer honoured. It becomes reduced to a mere stepping stone to the future, with no intrinsic value. Clock time then turns into psychological time [which is always linked to a false sense of identity].'

An important element of highlighting the Now, applying mindfulness, comes through concentrating totally on the particular moment or action – by putting our complete heart and soul into the activity. However small or apparently insignificant the action could be considered, we should still be giving it our full attention.

Example: Meaningful Menial Tasks

On many occasions in the past, I have been involved in filling envelopes with leaflets for largescale mailings – literally thousands of filled envelopes pile up on the tables which are transferred to postal boxes for delivery. You may have been involved in volunteering for similar activities. It's easy to see this as a mechanical task, but if you can maintain the attitude that each of these envelopes will be opened by an individual experiencing their Now moment, you will remind yourself of the importance of maintaining and checking standards as you prepare the filling for each envelope.

The positioning of each set of checked and correctly folded leaflets in each individual envelope then becomes your sequence of single Now moments, requiring total focus and concentration. It doesn't matter that some may be immediately consigned to the waste bin on receipt – it's the importance of the Now moment for those individuals reading the contents of their recently-received envelope which is the key issue.

If we're concentrating on what is happening Now – giving it our total focus of attention and accepting that we can create a brilliant outcome from it – we can enjoy the moment for what it is, absolutely making the most of it. Even if what we are able to offer is less than perfect on occasion, we can make something … the best we can … of it, in the belief that this has created the best Now experience possible for each recipient.

The Bigger Picture

On the other hand, when we're planning a bigger project, we'll probably have to subdivide it into several separate areas and consider these as a progression of events. Think about the different steps and stages along your development path. Doing this at such an early planning stage, gives you the chance to compare and contrast strategies you might use, while also helping you to see the chain of separate Now events more precisely.

Example: Becoming more Unselfish

Let's grasp a complex nettle and think of the objective of becoming a more selfless – or unselfish – person. Can we establish a totally final target for this? I don't think so! But we can perhaps see steps along a path disappearing towards the horizon. We could debate any sequence for days but one suggestion would be along the following steps.

- Think of a situation where you accepted decisions of others over your own
- What are a few personal standards which are very important to you?
- Review the extent to which you would compromise with each of these.
- What is the cut-off point for each, beyond which you wouldn't accept the situation?
- Think of an event where you conceded in favour of another
- How did you do it, to reduce any 'loss of face' for yourself?
- Think of situations where you have been helped by someone
- How did you ask for – and receive the help? Did you show gratitude?
- Identify some situations where you could help someone privately.

If you look at these different actions more closely, you should see that they break into separate groupings. Some join together in a logical sequence; others could be run in parallel. Sometimes, we could change the sequence of completing the different groups without harming the overall outcome. As we will establish later when we visualize our path along the track, our progress towards one particular goal or milestone can be blocked for a variety of reasons. If we've planned through sequences like this, it makes it easier for us to detour into another relevant activity and thus maintain progress.

Perhaps we should review the subtle difference of degree which is implicit in the adjectives 'unselfish' and 'selfless'. I'm not advocating that we're striving to become incredibly 'goody-goody' people, with no thought for ourselves. There will invariably be some good gained by ourselves in our actions – the point is that this becomes no longer our prime (or only) focus. As I understand the difference, we can make an unselfish decision, which will benefit others – but still have some consideration as to how the outcome will impact on ourselves. Selfless decisions have a higher degree of concern for others – I guess the ultimate would be where someone endangers (or ultimately sacrifices) his or her own life to save that of another. There are, of course, varying degrees of both selflessness and unselfishness! We're considering 'the bigger picture' and the potential benefits for others – if there's a 'spin-off benefit' for you, consider it as an added bonus!

It takes some time to appreciate the real benefits of thinking and planning in this way. It's worth persevering, though, because it will help you become more precise and confident when it's necessary to apply coping strategies to grasp those various nettles.

Everything is Relative

Maintaining an awareness of values helps us keep a handle on life. If we consider the world holistically and totally, many of our concerns shrink into insignificance. Is it important that we can't buy a particular bottle of wine when a complete African village is without water? Is it important that someone has hurt you by turning up late for a cinema outing when a whole country in the Middle East or Africa is at war with itself? Is some perceived slight from a friend really impossible to resolve, when the Israelis and Arabs will apparently be arguing about their different understandings of coexistence for ever?

Show a good example! If you've ever had a conversation with a Buddhist monk – or listened to the Dalai Lama speaking – you'll be aware that statements quite often end with a pause and laughter. It's their way of positively concluding statements on a particular matter. Also, they tend to pause and think, formulating their thoughts before speaking. We in the west feel less easy with silence, on occasion causing us to verbalize prematurely our randomly developing thoughts! If we can focus on the moment mindfully, peacefully and with consideration, we can keep our awareness of Now in perspective.

Meditation and MBCT

And so we come to meditation. In recent years, scientists have turned their attention to the effects of meditation and have now discovered that it has valuable, positive effects on the mind and body. Their studies of meditators have produced a whole literature and, by detailing changes in brain waves and which parts of the brain are called into operation during meditation, they have revolutionized what we know about the brain. They enable us to say with absolute certainty that meditation experience is real and has an effect on the whole bodily system and on our wellbeing. They have even discovered that the actual structure of the brain can be altered through regular deep meditation.

Now, you're probably wondering what MBCT means. It stands for Mindfulness-Based Cognitive Therapy – a therapy which has been created to counteract depression. In very simplistic terms, we could consider MBCT as a form of 'constructed' meditation. Encouraging empathy is one of the natural results of a true meditative state. Within MBCT practice, this encouragement has been established as an activity which can help lift people out of depression – so the outcomes and expectations of both are similar.

MBCT, in essence, trains people with depression to focus on what is happening in the moment – in the Now, one might say. Instead of dwelling on the past or future, which can encourage deepening depression, patients are shown how to focus on the Now, which helps them to improve their concentration and broaden their awareness of what is currently impacting their life. This mindfulness helps them to accept themselves for who they are, review and balance ego and control their awareness of others.

Practise, Practise, Practise…..

The message with MBCT training is that patients must practise it consistently – not just talk or read about it. The same is true for us developing mindfulness or meditation practices, in order to focus on the Now.

Think of the act, during meditation or mind focus, of gradually bringing your energy level down to a point of relaxation and reduced pace – finding that moment of inner peace. Your breathing gets deeper and more effective. Your mind empathizes more with humanity – in groups we become more entrained (or linked) with each other. This also involves getting progressively on the same 'wavelength' in terms of breath patterns – and even beliefs and understanding, over time. This can be facilitated greatly through certain vibrations in sound and music, which can encourage the Theta state which is beneficial to deep meditation – we will consider this a little further in chapter six.

A Return to Source

And so, in conclusion, we return to living in the Now and Mindfulness.

Mindfulness and meditation have no direct links with any religion – and should not really be described as religious practices. They can even be secular, a sort of secularized spirituality if you prefer – the application of a higher and more focused thought for the overall good. We can also accept that spirituality may exist happily outside any mainstream religion. Indeed, one might contend that spirituality (in the sense of being conscious of love in its broadest context, and displaying love to both oneself and others) actually remains freer to flourish outside the constraints of any organized religion.

A mindful, conscious attitude towards life can help us

focus deeply on the present moment of Now. Thinking in the Now will allow us to reduce the amount of stress potentially impacting upon us – and also allow us to cope positively with those periodic nettles which invade our path. Thinking in the Now is thus a valuable foundation for coping strategies.

Meditative Thought

The poem that follows considers a range of particular moments, with each one special in some unique way. It links rather effectively with our considerations of the Now.

Every Little Thing

Every victory leaves a taste of success;
Every journey has a path to pursue.
Each delight has a smile to be shared;
Each worry, some hope to renew.

Each new pain has a reason to exist,
To concentrate our thinking on the goal.
Every response has a modicum of hope ...
Of salvation, and development of soul.

Every new friend has a meaning to the bond:
Join hands, to eliminate the strife.
Each new encounter, a purpose if we seek ...
For progress – and a reason for our life.

Every sound has vibrations there to hear
In the mind of your heart, as it beats.
Each new thought, as it penetrates the mass,
Inspires us, our mission to complete.

Every thought has an element of truth.
If you contemplate the meaning and the sense
Each new song sends a rhythm to the soul,
Bringing influence and changes so immense.

Every instrument sends vibrations to the heart.
Every harmony brings senses to the ear;
Each combination gives a happiness inside
The listener, with stillness as they hear.

Every moment brings occasion for content;
Each experience, a chance for us to care.
Every thought has the purpose to succeed,
Each delight gives a smile – that we can share.

Chris Sangster

CHAPTER THREE

STRATEGIES FOR COPING: EMBRACING NETTLES GENTLY

S O, WHAT do we mean when we ask, 'are you coping?'? We cope with things in different ways – because these 'things' are different.

After acknowledging the success of the various medal-winners at the Olympics, we could ask each of these individuals how they were coping with their success. This, one would hope, would be a very positive form of coping. With some help and organization – and continuing motivation and training – many will make a lifetime career directly from their unique sporting success.

One could say that coping with winning the lottery might be along similar, positive lines. However, there are additional implications, largely based around the intelligent management (and potential redistribution) of money. Suddenly having apparently limitless amounts of money can confuse and corrupt the most sensible mind – and there have been documented cases of winners experiencing great difficulties in coping.

Example: Positive and Negative

From a totally different angle, we could be asking someone with cancer or undergoing intensive hospital treatment how they were coping. The hospital situation has more negative implications but doesn't need to have. After my relatively long spell in hospital, many people subsequently said to me, 'You must have been really frightened', 'You must have found it difficult to cope' or permutations of the same sentiment. In fact I didn't experience much fear or stress, because I took each day as it came, meditated a lot and developed a simple coping strategy (which we will consider, with others, in this chapter).

I've known several people with terminal cancer who have successfully taken each day at face value, trying to make it as normal as possible by doing things and going places within their current capabilities. We will be considering this in greater detail as we progress. It's another example of thinking in the Now.

Some Additional Crisis Situations Requiring Coping

Financial

Alongside cancer and other terminal illnesses, another crisis area requiring careful coping considerations is handling financial difficulties. They can be one of the lesser joys of self-employment, when the work dries up or there are delays in clients settling your invoices. And, in my experience, some client companies took pride in hanging onto their money for as long as possible – well beyond the expected thirty days from invoice tender! Coping with financial problems is a high-wire balancing act, reviewing priorities, delaying some payments, chasing possible income and so on – which again requires specific and unique coping strategies.

Family Life

Coping with bringing up children yet again requires different strategies, involving patience, understanding and the ability to communicate as they metamorphose through crying, simple but repetitive chatter, constant questioning, truculence, moody silences … and all the permutations between and beyond! Coping with any particular segment of the child's developing life will require specific strategies to meet that segment. Coping with the omnipresent needs of a crying baby, for example, is different from dealing with the stresses involved with a teenager who is threatening to 'go off the rails'.

One could go on. The major point being made, however, is that because we have a variety of situations we will be dealing with a range of strategies. Remember our equation,

$$CRISIS = SOURCE + CONCERNS$$

First, we must identify the source of the crisis in as clear detail as possible and then we can elaborate upon the various concerns which are troubling us. If we can identify professional support to address the source (to some greater degree at least), we can then focus on applying our strategies as appropriate, to relieve our concerns.

Living in the Now and Applying Forward Planning

We considered this to some degree earlier but we need to address this apparent contradiction more fully, before we progress any further.

When living and being in the Now, at its extreme you

will be conscious of neither past nor future. You will be focusing totally on the moment because it is of no immediate benefit to know what is to occur in the future – or indeed the outcomes of parallel actions in the past. Literally nothing else matters, at that particular moment in time. If this can be done successfully, you will experience less of the stress and fear, which would potentially be encouraged by your having this additional knowledge and awareness – which in turn could make it harder for you to cope).

I'm aware, of course, that the ability to switch off from fearful future imaginings will be harder for some people than others. I know individuals who, as well as automatically imagining that the worst will happen for any given scenario, will also consult the internet at great length to find out further possible effects and issues relating to their particular illness or problem.

They might reasonably see this research as a coping strategy in its own right, allowing them to know as much as they can about the illness, situation or whatever. With the help of the internet, my partner's sister had, as it turned out, diagnosed my illness before the specialists had reached agreement! So, research can help some people cope – just as long as the knowledge empowers them, rather than overwhelming them with additional fear and stress.

Normally, a focus on the 'Now' moment is likely to reduce or even eliminate fear and stress elements, as we will practise shortly. This is true for the more serious areas of coping outlined above. There are, of course, lesser degrees of coping, where positive future awareness does help. If the patient is aware of healing manifesting itself (where a swelling is visibly reducing or the act of swallowing is becoming easier, for example), looking towards improvement in the future becomes strongly motivating. (That's as long as the improvements are maintained, of course. Otherwise, concerns can resurface.)

Consider the uses of Now and the future as a sliding scale, based on how you can focus on what is immediately happening, coupled with the degree to which there is any positive benefit to you of being aware of future progressions.

Example: Terminal Illness

Even with what is apparently a totally negative situation, one in which we may be be coping by living very much in the Now, some knowledge of enjoyable activities in the future (such as a visit, an outing or a meeting with friends) gives milestones that enable us to see a positive, though finite life ahead. Anyone who has been involved, directly or indirectly, with the monthly chemotherapy process will know that it creates a cycle, with the 'S' curve rising to a high on the 'feeling crap' scale over the first couple of weeks, sinking to its best, relatively most normal point after about three weeks.

When Gillean was involved in this process, we sat down with the diary and planned out things which we could do together during the latter part of each four-week cycle of her chemotherapy treatments. This gave us positive milestones to motivate us in looking forward. In its earlier stages, plans included a stay in a luxury hotel in Thailand, where she insisted on us going on mountain-bike rides into the countryside – thus creating an additional concern I had to cope with! Our final holiday away, to a hotel near Glastonbury, involved a wheelchair for the first time. The medications became unstable during the final night there, which is always unsettling in an unfamiliar environment and, on our return, we agreed that holidays away from home would aggravate rather than relieve stressful concerns. The forward-planning process still continued to assist our daily 'Now' coping strategy, however, but with future milestones local and easier to cope with positively.

As a parallel, during the ten or so initial days I spent in hospital prior to being admitted to intensive care, I experienced some dramatic 'spikes' of fever, several of which I have since been informed were deemed life-threatening. The staff struggled to identify the obscure bacteria which were causing part of the problem and weren't responding to the range of antibiotics given to me in constant rotation. The specialist subsequently advised me, rather dramatically, that they had pulled me back from having 'one foot in the grave'. In this sense, my illness could also have been terminal – the difference was that I wasn't aware of the direness of my situation – and never doubted that I would improve.

So, on the other, more positive side of the cards, there can be increased benefits from being aware of possible future directional paths. We approached this earlier, when considering the benefits of having formulated Plans B and C and so on, rather than sticking blindly to Plan A when things start to go wrong. The subtle importance is that these plans are creating milestones and road markers that map out a potential choice of future directions. Then, when you reach a particular 'Now' moment where you experience a 'decision junction' in your journey forward, you can call up a range of possible options which you've previously considered – and can make informed decisions regarding onward direction more rapidly.

Planning Benefits

These subtle degrees of benefits in future planning might be summarized by saying:

- *Where knowledge of future outcomes can (rightly or wrongly) generate fear, it remains better to focus on the 'Now' moment as intensely as possible.*
- *Where awareness of alternative future strategies or results enables you to focus more confidently and objectively on each 'Now' moment as it occurs, this awareness is a benefit and should be incorporated.*

So, having established this sliding scale of involvement in future planning (with the same being true for incorporating past knowledge), we can now consider a range of strategies for coping with our concerns.

A Range of Coping Strategies

Strategy 1 – Controlled Breathing

One of the activities which features somewhere in virtually all coping strategies – but is also a strategy in its own right – is a focus on your breath. There's nothing magical about this – it's something internal to you and completely controllable by you; it's something you can focus on, without being reliant on any external factors – and the acts of deepening and slowing your breathing will have a direct effect on your metabolism. In stress-management terms, you will be allowing yourself to cope more easily.

In normal day-to-day existence, we tend to breathe quite shallowly, only using some fraction of our total lung capacity. If we bear in mind that the function of the lungs is to bring oxygen to our bloodstream and to expel the carbon dioxide for all those trees to soak up, the deeper we breathe, the more oxygenated the organs in our body will become.

Close your eyes (it's not really part of the process, but it helps you focus!) and concentrate on taking five slow, deep breaths, preferably breathing in through your nose and out through your mouth, watching the in- and outbreaths until they're comfortably complete. You'll probably feel slightly 'light-headed' at the end of this simple exercise, because your brain and body are receiving more oxygen than they're used to, so everything is functioning that little bit more effectively.

More Breathing

Now, try this extension to the exercise, to give you points of reference. When in breathing out you've reached the point where you would normally stop, keep on breathing out a little further, until you feel pressure on your diaphragm (towards the bottom of your chest). Hold it for a moment, and then breathe in through your nose, but this time continue taking air into your lungs until your chest begins to feel slightly painful with the added pressure. These then are the actual extremes of your lung capacity.

I'm not suggesting that you should normally breathe in and out to these extremes – but keep monitoring your 'normal' breathing rate periodically to ensure that you are extending and contracting your chest to the degree where you are oxygenating your body properly. When I was experiencing a feverish spike and focusing deeply on the Now in hospital, I periodically came to in the realization that I wasn't breathing at all – which was a bit of a surprise initially!

So, that's the physical action involved in breathing more effectively. How can this activity help you as a coping strategy?

- Firstly, it gives you an internal focus, to distract from your stress or pain
- It gives you the opportunity to slow down your pace of functioning
- It helps you get into a more relaxed, meditative state
- It allows you to think about your current 'Now' situation more objectively
- With eyes closed, it discourages others from interrupting your train of thought.

It's simple – but effective.

Strategy 2 – Using your Internal 'Slide Fader'

Perhaps you have seen (either for real or on television) the mixing desks that recording studios use. They have a battery of faders – which are the thumb controls which slide up and down to vary the volume of each track on a recording.

If you can visualize your body having a similar slide fader, you can begin to imagine that you can control the life forces or energies in your body. You might be able to visualize the fader in some way – if not, it doesn't really matter. Just imagine the effect of the fading action and go with it.

In the particular hospital example I've been mentioning, the need was to reduce the stress, concerns and fear associated with treatments, by sliding the fader down. In parallel situations, where I might want to boost my 'fight' response to deal with aggression or increase my outward confidence when talking in public, the visualization would evidently be increasing the fader. It can work both ways, depending on the situation with which you're attempting to cope. I'm sure other people must have used the same or similar techniques – but it certainly worked for me!

Example: Slide Fading as a Coping Strategy

I've never been very good with needles – I can't watch any-thing on the small or big screen that involves injections or surgery – and, when younger, I used to feel very faint every time the dentist gave me an injection prior to treatment. During my recent time in hospital – which amounted to twenty-six days – I was to have many injections, insertions of cannulas and PICC lines as well as various surgical inter-ventions while I was conscious. So, it became important for me to establish a means of coping with this.

The first element of the process was to get myself into a 'Now' state – thinking only of what was currently happen-ing – and not considering the implications of what might happen as a direct or indirect result. This was complicated prior to actual surgery as, when requiring you to sign the consent form, the surgeon rapidly listed all the possible side-effects if things went wrong (including, I recall, 'death', as I was lying on the operating table prior to a procedure under local anaesthetic to drain the chest cavity around my heart!). I just had faith that he knew what he was doing, signed, then focused on the moment once more!

So, I initially shut my eyes, concentrated on my breathing and imagined being surrounded by a protective bubble. Through practice, I managed to do this very rapidly – and then, into the imagined emptiness of my being, I visualized the slide fader inside me. As I breathed out, I could 'feel' this control sliding down inside my chest, apparently slowing down my vital energies and senses. As this happened, I felt my breathing slowing down and becoming shallower. I was, in effect, looking inward into my self and cutting off from the outward world and the procedure which was being performed. I was still conscious of the nurse or doctor being there, of course but it became almost as a disassociated party.

So, the stages can be summarized as:

- *Close your eyes and concentrate on your regular breathing*
- *Bring yourself to a 'Now' state, eliminating any thoughts of implications, effects etc*
- *Visualize yourself as protected by a bubble of white light, with mind evacuated*
- *Picture (in whatever way you can) a slide fader, operating on/in your chest*
- *Imagine this gradually sliding down, slowing down the vital energies*
- *Focus inwards, disassociating yourself from the procedure going on 'outside' you.*

It may sound a little 'other-worldly' – even slightly weird – but, with a little practice (and I certainly got lots of that!) it can become a coping strategy that has widespread application. I have used it in such diverse situations as sitting for long periods in an uncomfortable position; both 'shutting down' and rising to respond to discussions and arguments which I felt were not developing positively – with the up and down movement of the fader relating to whether or not I wanted to have further involvement in the discussion. I also use this control to filter out unwanted noise when trying to concentrate on something particular. Volume controls and slide faders are meaningful to me – you may find it more effective if you create a controlling image which is relevant to you, such as a tap, door or funnel. Try it, it does work!

Strategy 3 – *Applied Karma and Empowerment*
Karma is thought by some to be the law of 'cause and effect' – that there is a reason for everything happening, a cause

which you can respond to in a variety of ways but not evade totally. It links, to a greater or lesser extent, with many religions, with it being an overlying tenet with some. Even where this belief system is not present, I've found that many other people still believe in the effects of fate. So the general concept has varying degrees of effect in the thoughts and decisions of a wide range of people, yet I find that people understand – and apply – karmic principles in different ways.

At one extreme, the attitude is 'it's God's will and there's nothing I can do to affect it in any way'. I see this as being a bit like the example I mentioned earlier, of the sheep caught in the bramble thicket. An atmosphere of powerlessness and personal inactivity pervades, with the person more or less waiting to see the cards which life will deal him or her – almost as a punishment. Living in the Now – yes – but in a very neutral way.

At the other extreme, we have a belief that there are various milestones set out for us to address – but that we can have some say in how these are addressed. In 'business speak', this is often referred to as being 'pro-active': taking a hand in shaping how your life progresses. The successful attainment of these enabling milestones will mean that we can move ourselves onwards on our personal paths – called enlightenment by some. Any milestones (or personal remedial goals, if you prefer), which we do not approach successfully – or indeed bypass completely – will remain 'unfinished business', which will have to be readdressed at a later point, to achieve closure. A belief in reincarnation can help in the more detailed understanding and applications of this progress.

Between extremes, we have varying levels of self-empowerment and involvement, with each individual taking more or less control of the situation – or relying to a greater or lesser extent on the direction from others.

Deciding on the Degree of Decision-Making

So, we can identify those who are to some extent directed, maybe through an established religion or strong societal influences. Some individual decision-making may still be possible but this will often be shaped by established practices, laws and precepts. Variations will come about through the degrees to which individuals choose to follow the precepts they have accepted, within the reality of their lives.

The need to approach and respond to these requirements is not in question; nor is the need for us to get to each milestone successfully, in order that we may counter some previous action which is deemed to cause blockages along our path. It's the potential 'poor me, I'm a victim' attitude, which can become part of the process, which will often make it harder for the person to cope – largely because he or she feels, to some greater or lesser degree, powerless (taking on the mantle of victim).

It's particularly important that you don't see yourself as a victim caught up in your particular crisis. By practising the analytical processes we've discussed so far to identify sources, concerns and possible strategies, you can empower yourself to approach the crisis positively. You will then be more likely to be able to move forward towards resolving your concerns, with professional support as required to address the source.

Adding Empowerment

So, rather than having an attitude of powerless acquiescence, if we consider that we can maintain a role in deciding when and how we approach the required activity – especially the 'how' – we should immediately feel more in control and more capable of coping with the situation.

In virtually any situation, there will be some of the 'hows' that we'll never be able to control totally: availability of equipment, decisions from superiors (however inferior we consider these decisions to be!), time constraints, established procedures to be incorporated, health and safety requirements … the list could go on. We can often find some degree of flexibility, though, especially when dealing with more widespread issues.

Example: Managing Empowerment

Let's say your goal is to deal more positively and openly with people. Some of your attempts to achieve this will be more successful than others – because your actions and reactions will be coloured by the reciprocal actions and reactions of these people. This will evidently vary, so if you applied the same response, android-like, to each person, you're bound to be markedly more successful with some than others.

If you are feeling empowered, you would learn fairly rapidly through experience that you will have to gauge the attitudes and responses of each individual and adjust your methods of dealing with them accordingly. We will consider this in greater detail later. You will be responding to each situation because you feel that it's appropriate and possible to do so. And, by feeling positive in this way, you will succeed more effectively and probably faster.

How do you feel empowered? Some people achieve this through affirmations – through telling themselves that they are capable, by repeating motivational statements. There are many books and CDs giving examples of these. In my experience, they have a beneficial effect if done with consideration and thought. If done automatically, they probably have the equivalent effect to the mechanical 'high fiving' much-loved by wannabe sports personalities and other 'cool dudes'.

Some feel empowered through believing that they are capable of achieving – which must be based on some degree of competency, of course. Then, it's down to the power of positive thought. If you feel not only that you have the potential skills to do something but also that you have the capability to do it, you can do it. You may have to practise doing it – indeed you should practise it before going public – but the extra motivation of then doing it 'for real' will push your performance up those extra notches.

Part of this process is the stage of objectively reviewing your performance, identifying areas where you can improve for whatever reason – and coming up with strategies for improvement. Some can achieve this personally, while others need an external coach or mentor to discuss strategies. We all need this review process – empowerment is not a blind belief that we all know everything and can do everything. It's more a belief that we have the potential and certain skills which, through focus, belief and effort, we can bring forth effectively and successfully.

Watching an Olympic Games, we experience many races lasting literally minutes (or even seconds in some cases) – however, we are also reminded of of the many years of effort, endeavour, extreme training and ultimate selection on the part of the teams and individual athletes involved, which preceded the actual race. Compare this with many of the 'acts' who put themselves forward in TV talent shows – where we often witness hyperconfidence without many of the necessary associated skills. Empowerment doesn't inevitably come easily!

So, if we can feel that we have some say in how we carry out our karmic responsibilities, we should feel in a stronger position to cope with our various concerns linked with each crisis, no longer considering ourselves to be the victim.

Strategy 4 – Embracing the Nettles of Life – Literally

Let's start off with considering the activity literally! When we lived up in Scotland, I experienced a fairly outdoor life, with land and sheep to maintain and a holiday cottage business to service. Unfortunately, all this manual activity gradually manifested itself in arthritis in my hands.

One of the natural 'cures' which was suggested to counteract arthritis was using stinging nettles. These plants (from the species urtica) are covered in tiny hairs, which are in effect silica tubes with toxins in a sack at the base. When we press against them, the tops of the tubes snap off and the toxins shoot into the penetrated skin, causing pain and a short-term rash. Think of a combination of glass phial and syringe and you've got the effect! Nonetheless, the toxins are considered to act both as a diuretic and to ease joint pain, probably by reducing the levels of inflammatory chemicals around the joints. The effects of the toxins may even change the way the body transmits pain signals.

I tried this for a while, finding that brushing my hands through nettle beds gave more of a stinging effect to the affected area of the hands than grabbing the nettle tightly. Grabbing or grasping a nettle (or indeed a problem) takes more nerve, however, as one is in effect approaching and tackling the potential aggressor head on. The act of embracing a group or patch of nettles – sweeping them aside with a covered arm – gave added protection and usually resulted in an easier outcome. You may note the subtle rash of life-parallels creeping in there!

Embracing the Nettles – more Figuratively

So, gently dealing with the varied nettles of life needs a bit of knowledge, a degree of nerve … and may result in a bit of short-term surface pain. The act of openly embracing the nettle can, however, reduce the feelings of internal pain, at least temporarily. At its extreme, it can change situations for the better, (where, in extremis, the nettle was not only embraced but grasped firmly and pulled up). Notice, once again, that the action in the physical context is easing joint pain (arguably!) but can not be considered to be a healing process (in any sense of permanent repair). Although the arthritic body is not healed, the mind is encouraged to think positively that some improvement is possible. In more general terms, embracing and responding positively to problems can certainly improve the situation – but it might need ongoing efforts to maintain the progress. To respond so positively is also, however, a form of living in the Now, so it is a little more than just something providing temporary relief.

Applying this coping process generally depends on a variety of things. You must:

- be aware of the type of problem you're approaching
- be confident that there are strategies available which can be applied
- be aware of – or consider – the detail of these possible strategies
- feel that any initial pain (in the broadest sense) is worth it for the subsequent gain
- feel empowered by the belief that firm action can change matters for

the better

- take the first step towards action confidently, once a strategy has been decided.

Example: Persevering with an Action you Believe in

While we were living in Wiltshire, Gillean and I made a trip to Scotland, one of our projects being to walk on the Knoydart peninsula, which is accessed up a single-track road of twenty-plus miles, past Loch Garry. When driving, we passed a lovely white shooting lodge, which was then a hotel. Gil fell in love with it on sight and, when we subsequently decided to move to Scotland to run a holiday cottage business, we were clear that we wanted to buy it. We'd already stayed in the hotel on several trips, checking out discretely how the building could be subdivided, to make several terraced cottage units, plus a main house section for ourselves. I had also introduced the owner to the possibility of selling it to us.

Not wanting to put all our eggs in the one basket, we visited other suitable properties in the area during each trip – but these, in all truth, only served to underline the perfection that the property represented. We were set on moving, however, so if negotiations had collapsed, we would have bought something else – we had several Plan Bs but would have been slightly disappointed in any one of them. Negotiations continued over almost two years, until we were talking amounts of money that we could see seriously interested the owner – and which we knew would be more than covered by the sale of our home in Wiltshire, which was a substantial old manor house.

Even after agreeing on the sale, there was a major amount

of fine-detail negotiations regarding land, water and fishing rights and so on to complete, with our written communications becoming quite stressful at times because of changes of mind between phone discussions and written confirmations. Gillean and I never really faltered in our belief that we would complete the purchase, however, and had clear plans of how we were going to convert the buildings, even before we set foot in them as owners.

Many people we knew felt that there was no chance that the owners would sell – and that we were fools setting up in a business in which we'd had no major experience. We grasped the nettle, being fully convinced that we would manage. And manage we did, creating a traditional-style environment that enticed many visitors back as regulars, and we sold it seven years later for a lot more than we paid for it. We also had some wonderfully enjoyable experiences in Scotland – and as an offshoot, Gillean wrote a book entitled HOW TO START AND RUN A HOLIDAY COTTAGE BUSINESS, which still sells as one of the trade's standard reference books. So, our confidence paid off!

Money Matters

Financial problems are like bellyache – once you have them, they keep nagging away, often getting progressively worse until ultimately faced up to and tackled. Coping with financial problems is a multifaceted activity. I'm by no means a financial expert, so the first bit of advice I would give is, as soon as you feel things sliding, get in touch with a financial person and talk through the problems.

Don't do it with a view to getting loans (or, worse still, additional loans) but as a means of reviewing any income and all outgoings. Sadly, in this current climate, you might argue that some European countries are keeping themselves going in an identical way (taking on new loans to pay the interest on previous loans) but it doesn't need much financial acumen to realize both the short- and longterm foolishness of these stabs at salvation.

Here, we have another angle of the Now and the future, bearing in mind that it's likely that the past actions have created the problem to some extent. Not necessarily knowingly, however. It seems perfectly manageable to be paying out around £200 per month on a new car purchase scheme, when the monthly salary cheque continues to pay into your account. Paying £200 takes on a different challenge if the job and salary suddenly dry up and the purchase contract has still months or years to run.

Around fifty years ago, when it was 'hire purchase' rather than 'credit', there was still a strong ethos among many that you saved up to buy something, rather than 'getting into debt'. It's not our place here to debate the pros and cons of the changed attitude towards debt and the proliferation of store cards. Acceptable levels of debt will vary between countries but it's disturbing to read that the average amount owed per UK adult (including mortgages) in early 2012 was well over £29,000. This is, apparently, around 120% of average earnings! It doesn't take much of a financial brain to realize that therein lies a problem, both for the Now and the future.

Strategy 5 – Coping with Finances

Considering the Now – this moment in time (or the point in this financial month for this example) – we should have an awareness of expected income and expenditure. As mentioned earlier, this takes on an added complexity where income is not regular, in timing or amount (or both). To varying degrees, we have some control of expenditure, in terms of the extras which we may elect to buy. This is where 'credit card mentality' (debts not paid off monthly) can muddy the pool – and where personal debts begin to grow.

OK, there are particular times of the year where expenditure does shoot up – largely around Christmas and the summer holiday period. I worked for several years in Belgium, where they actually had a universal system (which I believe they may still use) where the annual salary was divided by fourteen rather than twelve, giving you less on a monthly basis but double salary twice a year – a built-in savings plan, which seemed a very good idea. It may seem slightly boring, but the best starting point for coping financially must be to review carefully whether each new purchase is affordable. If you pay off your credit card bill every month, this gives an extra flexibility for a month (or longer, if you time your purchases carefully). Overall, however, you're still trying to live within your means.

Then there are of course the regular expenditures, like utilities, food, petrol and other regular but necessary outgoings. These too can be controlled at source – buying produce for cooking rather than ready-prepared meals or takeaways; not leaving lights on in empty rooms; turning down central heating thermostats; planning car journeys to make best use of the visit to town and so on. All these help to reduce the bills and assist with financial coping strategies before they get a chance to get out of hand. The real starting point for managing your concerns is to be careful and considerate about how you consume services and utilities – 'control expenditure at source' is a good place to start.

Income Drought

The real crisis requiring strategic coping comes where income dries up. However careful you have been with controlling your expenditure, it's still there and the bills need paying. It's often reckoned that you should have savings equivalent to at least two months' salary, in order to cope with short-term redundancy. Unfortunately, in the current climate, this short-term nature of unemployment is no longer guaranteed, raising the bar somewhat. Even though you may have built up some level of financial buffer (or receive a redundancy payment that seems large on the face of it), this will diminish quite rapidly, where there is no ongoing income to replenish the coffers. 'Something will come up' may work in spiritual circles – I've seen monasteries and similar buildings being funded on this focused belief – but it's not a key coping strategy for personal financial difficulties!

Financial Specialists

'Go and talk to the specialists' is a much better strategy – your bank, the citizens' advice bureau or others who can help you to prioritize payments and negotiate with your creditors. You need to review your current commitments – that shiny new car may have to go back; the expensive holiday may need cancelling (you did take out insurance, I hope!); the kids might need to do without their sports and music coaching … they'll survive! And you need to find any means of gaining an income, however small and irregular.

What you don't want to do as a coping strategy is to start taking out loans from high-interest providers, in order to maintain outward appearances and pretend that the problem's not there. It won't go away and the debts will just continue to mount, until your situation becomes untenable. There are various strategies available nowadays for repackaging and paying off debt. Some might appear rather unfair to the creditors involved but that's a moral decision you must take. Talk to the mainstream specialists – they'll help you cope.

Strategy 6 – Coping with Family Matters

Having and raising a family needs an immense amount of ongoing coping – and nothing quite prepares you for the wide range of concerns which can upset you along the way. In the years following the birth of a child, inexplicable crying, sleepless nights and the sheer omnipresence of the new little presence can't help but catch the parent unawares, especially with the first child. Gone are the moments when you can do things spontaneously such as pop out to the shops, or the pub, and a brain which has had years of working at an advanced level in some professional situation becomes largely preoccupied with relieving crying, feeding and changing nappies. It's a wonderful experience overall, of course, and a marvel to watch children develop, but there are certainly many challenges along the way to cope with.

The developing years give the parents the opportunity to create the behavioural foundations which the child will build on – and upon which the parents can set the guidelines and parameters. In recent years, the media, peer-group pressures and social networking have made this much more of a minefield in which to cope. To some large degree, this is because of the difficulties in maintaining an oversight and control which is inherent in the computer age – when a 2009 ChildWise report revealed that children spend on average around six hours a day viewing the screen, whether as TV, computer games or the internet. Some surveys have the figure much higher.

The teenage years become even more complicated, with lack of real communication a potential stumbling block between monosyllabic youth and preoccupied parents. There are exceptions, of course, but addressing communication – or just spending time together – can help. The decline in the ritual of families eating together at the dining table (indeed the reduction in the number of households actually owning a dining table!) is a direct indicator of the lack of quality contact time in the average family. Family members are a lot more likely to 'snack' individually while watching TV. This can be a direct result of the number of extra-curricular sport and other activities occupying each child, which are intrinsically good but less so if fragmenting the nuclear unit of the family. When the hours away from the family home are spent 'hanging out' with mates, without any real direction or purpose, it can lead to even greater fragmentation.

These are of course the more negative aspects – there can, in addition, be wonderful and positive experiences in growing and developing a family – but we are considering the coping strategies here. Added complications can arise where the marriage has broken down and the children are being brought up by one parent. That's perfectly possible, of course, and there will be many cases where the atmosphere is more stable than where two feuding parents are present in the household. But it can put greater stresses on coping with the upbringing of hormonally-active teenagers.

Criteria for Coping with Children's Maturation

- Take time to communicate – listening as well as talking
- Discuss and set 'house rules' and stick to them
- Monitor computer use – try to understand the technology
- Have 'family times' together to share thoughts and experiences
- Encourage children to have active part in household chores
- Pocket money should be earned in some way – not a handout
- Monitor and seek detail of content of homework – offer help if needed
- Focus on the Now, with reference to the future as positive plans
- Allow children to learn positively from the past – don't reopen blame scenarios
- Offer your experience in an open way, to help them look to the future.

There are, of course, many other situations within family life which can create crises. Alcoholism, violence, abuse and other such situations all create their own particular crises, major ones that must be dealt with very specifically and with great care. Although it is not the remit of this book to delve into such complex and unique problems, there is (thankfully) a full range of support agencies in most western countries, where particular assistance can be sought.

Strategy 7 – Isolating Source and Concern
We have been reviewing and applying this consistently so far but it should feature as one of the strategies, for future cross-reference.

Once again, consider the equation:

$$CRISIS = SOURCE + CONCERNS$$

Because we're more likely to be able to address the concerns by applying the strategies we've been discussing, we want to isolate these. This can happen more easily if we have first identified the source of our crisis as clearly as possible.

As we've been reinforcing consistently, once the source has been identified, we can further identify external professionals who can help us tackle that particular problem. Thenceforth, we will be freer to focus on considering our concerns.

Example: the Initial Stages of my Illness

As often happens at the onset of illness, I had been nursing a sore throat for several days, in the expectation that it would get better, and with the administration of lozenges and hot drinks. The weekend came – in this case it was a holiday weekend – and on the Saturday I remained in bed as the throat was getting worse. I put on extra bedclothes and wrapped a scarf round my throat, as I was beginning to shiver. (Wrong move, as I discovered later. Fevered shivering is a sign of higher temperature spikes, not coldness).

On the Sunday, matters were worse and we managed to go along to an emergency clinic fifteen miles away, where a doctor examined me and gave me a programme of standard penicillin-type antibiotics to take.

So far, then, we'd identified the source as a 'sore throat' and managed to get medical treatment as a response. Things would now improve (we thought), so our concerns were alleviating.

However, after a fitful Sunday night, there was little change – but we thought it was just a case of waiting for the antibiotics to kick in. That is, the results of professional help should soon manifest itself. There was a growing concern, however, as I was finding it increasingly hard to swallow.

This continued through Monday day and night. (In hindsight, we should have presented ourselves at the Emergency Department of the hospital at this point – but still had faith in the antibiotics working and didn't want to 'be a trouble'!)

On Tuesday morning, with my local doctor's surgery open once more at 8.30 a.m., I hit the telephone booking system and, after the usual fifteen minutes of continuous dialling and redialling, got an appointment for 4.30 that afternoon. By this time, my throat was worse and I was really feeling feverish, with my concerns growing higher again. We had established the source (a sore throat and fever) but it was becoming apparent that the professional response wasn't working. An hour later, my partner phoned the surgery and it was agreed that I should go down then.

Two doctors had a look at me – and were rather shocked when they saw my distended and discoloured neck when I removed the scarf (which I'd worn constantly over the weekend – not a shrewd move as I reckon it had helped to incubate the bacteria). An ECG showed up an irregular heartbeat – and next thing I knew, I was being helped into an ambulance. I felt I was in good professional hands then, so my concerns abated somewhat (little did I know at this point that I had almost a month's worth of hospital treatment ahead of me!)

So, I'll stop at this point. Notice the fluctuations in awareness and belief of the source of the crisis, the professional support and the related concerns. As a postscript, it took the hospital eleven further days of exploratory treatment to identify one of the (very rare) bacteria present in my system and locate a form of antibiotic which would have an effect. I received massive doses of this and conventional antibiotics over a total period of seven weeks, both intravenously and in capsule form after being discharged.

This example, with its fluctuations, illustrates the variable nature of some crises, where concerns will rise and fall and professional responses will not necessarily solve the problem instantly (if at all – sometimes, alternative professional responses will need to be sourced and applied). Overall, it does however illustrate the benefits of isolating the source, in order that concerns can be better managed.

Summary

There are thus a variety of different strategies which can be applied – either as individual activities or through combinations, to meet particular requirements. Sometimes, the best strategy is to focus very much on the Now moment – in other situations, some vision of the future will help to evaluate possible, alternative solutions, preparing us for rapid decision-making should a solution be required later. As each situation, to some great extent, will be unique, approach it with an open mind, rather than trying to shoehorn situations into particular pre-solutions.

Although we have reviewed a relatively wide range of coping areas, many of the situations we'll be considering in subsequent chapters will be focusing on your personal needs, such as illness, stress and inter-relationships with others, so we should now progress to considering how healing in its broadest sense can help.

Meditative Thought

The following poem gives an example of individual coping which is particularly hard to bear – and which takes a lot of courage and lateral thinking to overcome. It relies to a great extent on focusing on the Now, with any recurring memories from the past being exceedingly hard to bear, for many months or even years after the death. The memories and grief can be triggered by the simplest of things – a song, a view, a scent, an atmosphere – and need release to alleviate stressful build-up of energies.

The Widower

Newspaper read from start to end
Though detail quite forgotten now;
Obituary that told her tale
Long gone – and now he wonders how
New days can be, with thought and sigh,
As empty chair reminds the past,
Of happy times, the talk and smiles –
Activities they dreamed would last

The garden walked, in mournful thought
With weeds where once was verdant soil;
The plans for borders, shrubs and trees
Now withered, lacking hopeful toil.
Her spade lies rusting by the shed,
Its use no longer he can bear;
The brambles' arms reach out to grasp,
But he can neither hope nor care.

Habitual seat is cold, forlorn;
One table setting, or of late

Cold comfort balanced on a tray
With TV host his only mate,
But conversation is one-way:
His comments fall on empty ears –
No longer can he voice his joys,
His hopes, his musings – or his fears.

As times go past and tensions ease
Some hope flares up for consort new,
No mirror image – but at same
Time, showing traits that they held true.
The internet and lonely hearts,
Through columns deep he wades in trust
Creative wording dulls the search –
Where love is sought for, only lust.

Then chance encounter, interests bond
A new relationship takes flight
In love resembling; aspects new
Come to the fore, on that first night.
The table set, the garden blooms
Close chats while walking in the lanes,
A second chance he grasps with joy
Walks happy in the world again.

Chris Sangster

CHAPTER FOUR

HELP FROM HEALING PROCESSES

What is Healing?

WHEN I found myself in hospital, I experienced a wonderful rush of people offering to send me healing, through prayer, meditation, healing groups – or, more generally, through positive thought. Having made something of a study of its effects over the years and because, prior to admission to hospital, I had been studying applications of healing through sound and music extensively, it was interesting to be involved from the other side of the fence, so to speak, as a patient rather than a healer. Direct involvement does help to focus the mind and re-evaluate priorities!

Vibrations and Healing

There are countless complementary therapies available for healing, in the broadest sense of the word and, as with spiritual healing, many work very effectively for some people. As well as the 'hands-on' techniques such as massage, reiki and contact healing, we find a wide range of treatments, including Chinese medicine and homeopathy. Personally, I had become increasingly involved in various sound therapy activities, applying sound vibrations from instruments including the gong, singing bowl, tuning fork and shamanic drum, so it was interesting to review the perceived effects of these various options while in my hospital bed! It's undoubtedly true that healing in the sense of relaxation, stress-release or a generally positive raising of the life-force (also referred to as *chi* or *prana*) can happen where the patient has a positive expectation of improvement. Different treatments will, of course, work better for some than others. Over the years as a patient I personally never gained much success from homeopathy but Gil had an almost miraculous cure from very serious migraine attacks, thanks to homeopathic analysis and treatment using essence of iris. There are many absent healing groups who meet to transmit healing energy to patients who are consciously on the group lists of patients – and who gain positive healing from this consciousness.

Example: Healing and Cancer

Having lost several close family members to various forms of cancer, I would perhaps question what the actual perceived meaning and outcome of 'healing' is. It was perhaps a sign of our naivety – or lack of informed support – but, after drug treatment and surgery in Wiltshire, Gillean and I genuinely believed that her cancer was 'healed'. It was only when it returned during our time in Scotland, that the concept of it having merely been 'in remission' was expressed, with some incredulity that we weren't aware of this. We were not conscious of anyone having explained this to us and, as can happen in such situations, there was perhaps a blindly optimistic attitude on our part.

As tends to happen with such illnesses, Gil had read about someone who had, through special holistic treatment,

been healed of various brain tumours and other cancerous
growths – with there being no doubt in that patient's mind
(certainly at the time when the article was written) that this
healing was seen as being a permanent 'cure'. One invariably hears or reads about these cases, and it carries the danger
that, with a degree of desperation, the exceptions can easily
be seen as the rule. As well as electing to receive alternative
treatment over several years (alongside conventional medical interventions), Gil latterly also had regular contact healing in a centre near our new home in Hampshire, when we
subsequently moved to be nearer the family.

Returning to our equation –

$$CRISIS = SOURCE + CONCERNS$$

– this range of responses, treatments and interventions certainly helped with healing psychologically, in the sense of
calming both concerns and related stress. It is evidently difficult to gauge the effectiveness of actual medical healing
in what is deemed to be a 'terminal illness'. Being realistic, we are looking more for a meaningful extension to the
life, rather than expecting a cure. The ultimate response, to
which there is no real answer, can of course be that the patient might have died earlier, if the range of treatments had
not been followed. The degree of intervention applied is a
moral dilemma, ultimately down to the patient to consider
and review, if capable – with input from direct relations and
professionals.

Involvement in one's healing processes becomes both
part of the steps towards positive improvement and a focus
for the various minds involved in the process. It can take
over the major proportion of each day, following proce-

dures, treatments and research – to the point where there is little time left for day-to-day living. As I outlined earlier, we planned out future activities and outings to coincide with the peaks and troughs of chemotherapy, to make the most of life and experiences when we could. So, a degree of involvement in – and control of – the overall process certainly helps the overall healing in the psychological sense, bringing composure and a degree of inner peace.

Example: The Carer's Perspective

Speaking from personal experience, it can be potentially difficult for any carer to maintain enthusiastic support during this overall process. The carer will have his or her own views about the effectiveness – or even validity – of some of the healing procedures, but must acknowledge any positive psychological benefits gained by the patient. Beliefs can be further complicated by the not-inconsiderable cost involved when seeking additional private treatments or drugs, some of which may still be at an experimental stage. The key responsibility of the carer must be to remain as positive as humanly possible, in the eyes of the patient.

Taking life as it came, Gil and I managed to have some wonderful experiences in our last year or so together. Though threatened by many and varied figurative nettles, potentially causing pain and sadness, we managed to grasp each situation as it evolved, make the most of it and share our remaining times as happily as possible.

The 24/7 nature of caring for a relation – as opposed to professional caring, where time with any one patient is likely to be more limited – makes it harder for both parties to remain upbeat. There is perhaps a tendency for the carer to become very stoical, not wishing to ask for help or relief from 'outsiders' and being very patient-focused. If you want to test this, ask any carer how he or she is. Invariably, after one or two generalized sentences, the carer will be speaking about the patient's condition, not their own! If you are aware of people caring for a relative, can I say on their behalf that it is wonderful having time off for a break, personal activity – or even a total, uninterrupted rest, so please consider offering to stand in for a few hours, whether they ask or not!

Healing as Improved Attitude

In September 2008, I became a widower, so healing in the medical sense had evidently not taken place. But healing in the positive, attitudinal sense, in the sense that Gillean felt positive hope in the future, however long or short this would be, certainly created the belief and physical strength which allowed us to experience those wonderful things and activities, almost until the day of her death.

Ironically, my brother went through a very similar process of maintaining interest and activity during his cancer treatment. He was actually out at someone's seventieth birthday celebration the day he died! In both cases, a positive and involved approach to their situations helped them deal with life's nettles with interest and hope, with this participation improving greatly the attitudes of both themselves and those around them.

The death of my wife and brother (followed closely by my dog, a collie named Star, with whom I'd worked closely for years) were all areas of coping for which I had to apply personal   strategies. In each case, to varying degrees, my coping was helped by the fact that I was consciously putting my efforts into supporting the other party's healing endeavours. Although this positive involvement initially helped in facing each death, subsequent private grief gave some personal relief, again helped by the 'slide fader' process.

I have thus absolutely no doubts that healing in the sense of encouraging positive thinking, bringing peace to the soul and engendering confidence in being able to cope with the situation is immensely beneficial. As patients – and indeed carers – we need as much support as possible in achieving this, from as many sources as are available.

The Mind is its Own Place

My father used to quote the lines from Milton's poem, *Paradise Lost*, that read:

> *The mind is its own place, and in itself*
> *Can make a Heaven of Hell, a Hell of Heaven.*

Although it expresses the extremes, I personally find that there can be a lot of truth in this comment. Receiving healing in the sense of hope, encouragement and a feeling that there is still potential in life to do things, regardless of the degree of medical condition, is indeed making 'a Heaven of Hell', to some degree.

In this sense, there is perhaps a subdivision between healing as meaning restoring the body to a totally healthy state and healing as meaning focusing on the reduction (or even the localized elimination of) pain, concerns and fear associated with the source illness. In doing this, the aim is to allow some attempt at living a more normal life in the Now. This is another example of gently embracing the nettle: not to pull it out (which would require greater effort and interventions) but more to turn it aside, to allow us to experience a continued, positive existence while we remain capable of applying it.

In spiritual healing, there is the understanding that all cells in our bodies regenerate, with every cell subject to 'divine power and glory'. This of course implies that the regenerated cell is new and healthy, which is unfortunately not demonstrably the case with the likes of cancer – or indeed the septic puss which accumulated in my neck cavity, requiring surgery to eliminate.

Combating these complex situations requires a holistic approach, with a combination of medical, spiritual and even psychological interventions for the patient to potentially re-enter a stable state. The absence of any one of these can prolong the period of disease and can, of course, lead to graver complications.

Bell Curves and the Ageing Process of the Body

There is a theory that many situations and processes in life follow a natural growth and decay curve in the shape of a bell. Things will naturally improve or develop to a point where they reach the top of the curve, and then will naturally begin to decay. This decline shows as a mirror image of the curve – creating the bell shape. So attempting to maintain a line from the top of the curve, continuing horizontally, becomes increasingly hard, if not impossible. This is natural law, with some people describing similar bell curves for areas as diverse as the growth and decline of a business, the increasing maintenance needs of an ageing building or the productivity of land which has been over-farmed without proper nutrition.

The bell curve concept is also represented in the way the body progresses through youth, maturity, age and decay. Like the ageing building, our bodies experience increased problems in trying to maintain continued 'horizontal' physical and structural standards, when our physiology is tending towards following the natural decline of the curve.

So, perhaps we need to reconsider our definition of healing – becoming that of generating a more positive response to overcoming the concerns and pains caused by the illness – rather than necessarily correcting the source illness itself. This, in turn, links with our belief in thinking in the Now and not dwelling on future twists and turns. Having had an illness, especially a life-threatening one, the patient is aware of the symptoms which preceded the illness – and the stages of the illness itself (coupled with the interventions). Where there is subsequently any recurrence of any of these symptoms – real or imagined – the future fear element is more likely to kick in, aggravating the symptoms. The patient is distracted by what might happen in the future, rather than focusing on what can be done to help matters in the Now. Although some element of fear of the future might act to make the patient more careful in the present, too much will certainly make matters worse.

Example: the Caring Carer

There was a television programme recently where TV personalities (themselves pensioners) spent time working with

individual pensioners who had been identified as having particular issues. One case involved a bedridden man who was
being cared for by his wife. The situation started with him refusing to go into a respite home for a week or two – because
he was afraid he would be left there permanently. Meanwhile,
his wife was desperate for a break, with exhaustion making
her level of caring more and more automatic. By the time the
programme-makers approached them, the level of communication between the two had deteriorated to a level where the
patient was in a depressed, monosyllabic state, while the carer
was permanently near to tears with frustration.

Through the freshness of a third-party 'go-between'
(coupled no doubt with the motivational magic of the presence of TV cameras!), the man was persuaded that his wife
would not leave him in the respite home permanently –
which is not the function of respite homes anyway. With
the help of a relation coming in to 'patient sit', the wife and
the TV personality went out to Bingo for an evening off –
the first for a very long time. By chance (or through a little
magic of TV influence, perhaps!) the wife won the jackpot
of over one thousand pounds, making her dream of going
on a cruise a possible reality.

This is all a necessary preamble to the healing part of the
story. The three got together for a discussion, culminating
in the man realizing that his thoughts of being left were ir-
rational and agreeing to enter the respite home to allow his
wife to go on the cruise. The healed atmosphere between
the two – manifesting as an outpouring of relief and honesty – was wonderful to experience. The bedridden husband
was able to verbalize his frustrations at being so dependent
on his wife, which had manifested as silent mood-swings,
while the wife spoke about her guilt at increasingly treat-

ing him as an object rather than a person. His illness had not improved medically but the contact, emanations of love and depth of understanding between the two had healed immeasurably. I can only imagine that, on coming together after their break and relaxation in new environments, their bond together regained some of its former enthusiasm.

Although there was no identified improvement in the source illness, the additional source problem – the breakdown in communication, trust and outward demonstrativeness, which had burgeoned to create these various concerns – had been addressed very effectively.

The Ayurvedic Approach

Ayurveda, which originated in India, considers health and illness in a holistic way – an approach which the west is belatedly attempting to follow to some extent. It considers each patient's personality and personal qualities, and his or her environmental situation and other individual issues, as well as the actual medical condition. It has been known to be successful where a more conventional approach has failed to achieve a response.

Through analysing the individual patient in an initial consultation, the ayurvedic doctor can identify the patient's primary characteristics – which will have an impact on how he or she reacts to the selected approach to treatment. Analysis is based round different bio-energies – *vatha, pitta* and *kapha*. Perhaps, as it's a lesser-known approach in the West, I will include slightly more detail than with other approaches documented here.

- Vatha *responds to the basic elements of ether and air, giving dry, cold and clear characteristics.*

- Pitta *responds to the basic element of fire, giving hot, mobile and sharp characteristics*
- Kapha *responds to water and earth, giving oily, cold, immobile and soft characteristics.*

One can be diagnosed as having a combination of these bio-energies, with treatments selected to counteract an out of balance bio-energy. To take a simplistic example, rheumatism can be traced to a hyperactive *vatha* (dry, cold and penetrating). Heat would therefore be a counteracting response, giving heat therapy as a preferred treatment.

The system is very complex – with each of the bio-energies split into several different sub-degrees – and requires many years of study and application. The prognosis will cover not only medical aspects but also diet and digestion processes, times of day where each identified energy may be expected to be hyperactive, mood indicators and even the weather. There are many books written on the subject, for those who might wish to study the detail further – the interesting angle on the whole subject is its holistic nature, requiring an initial, in-depth consideration of the person and his or her circumstances, diet and environment as well as the illness. This can create a much more detailed understanding of the source of any medical imbalance – with analysed and prescribed responses likely to allay concerns to a high degree.

Summary: Help from Healing Processes

We can approach healing processes from several different angles – medical, spiritual and psychological, with an individualized holistic combination being the best response to meet particular cases. As with many two-way situations, the needs and expectations of the receiver are as important as those of the giver, for optimum effect. Nowhere was this more apparent than in the initial Ayurvedic consultation mentioned above: a degree of interpersonal contact that western medicine could benefit from emulating to a greater degree.

A favourite question asked by medical staff in hospital is 'on a scale of one to ten, how would you rate your pain level?' This gives a reference marker – if rather a subjective one, which could also be applied to perceived degrees of healing. I have been asked by various people if I am '100% (or completely) better'. How can you gauge that, given that there are side-effects of surgery, physical weight-loss and often ongoing discomfort in the Now – and the latent fear of recurrence remains, if one dwells on the past and future?

There are many nettles and many ways and degrees of embracing them – the secret perhaps is to spend time initially analysing the best response to any given situation. The majority of medical interventions I have experienced have left some traces of pain and discomfort with which I have had to cope. In all cases, the remaining traces can be considered to be minor compared with the original source of each related problem, so this positive response helps to underpin selected coping strategies!

Meditative Thought

The following poem acts as a summary of the key thrust of this chapter – that the healing energy can be transferred by a variety of methods and techniques, to benefit each patient in a way which is conducive to his or her particular needs.

It also underlines the key point made in the chapter – that healing is a wider concept than merely mending the body; sometimes the healing is of the mind or spirit, which can be equally beneficial.

Now it's Healing

The touch which comes from healing light
Brings aid when pain besets the mind;
Strong pulses flow through chakras bright –
A true response, relief to find.

With eyes firm closed the patient waits;
The healing flows, from groups around,
As absent healers, powers innate,
Spread love to many, hopes abound.

On stool or couch the patient seeks
The healing touch, to ease the pain
That comes from past or future fate.
Focus on Now, respite to gain.

Now is the time, the guru says,
When faith will bring the healing through
To mind and soul, for he who prays;
Though body frail, belief is true.

The carer's focus on the needs
Gives help where patient's hope aspires,

Through conscious love and selfless deeds
The body rallies, sense on fire.

So healing can be heart or head:
Sometimes response evades the goal
To heal the body, but instead
We find the answer in the soul.

Chris Sangster

CHAPTER FIVE

HARNESSING THE LIGHT OF LOVE

A S THE SONG says, 'What's love all about?' Check in a thesaurus and synonyms are wide and varied – they include adulation, affection, ardour, attachment, devotion, fondness, friendship, liking, partiality, passion, regard, respect, and warmth.

If we take the generally-considered amorous relationship between two (or more) people, we are in no doubt about the accepted meanings of the likes of affection, ardour, fondness, passion and regard. But what about the applications of love in the broader setting – in day-to-day living and working and coping with each other? How do we apply the principles in this wider context?

One of the most profound – but also simple – tenets of wisdom for us to apply as widely as possible is that of loving others, in the broadest sense of the word. As Jesus said, 'Love thy neighbour as thyself'. It's simple – 'Do as you would be done by' conjures up the same sentiment. Act in the same way; say the same types of things and work to the same standards that you would genuinely expect others to apply to you. Having established these guidelines, you can then use them as a set of criteria against which to match your every action. That's what love's all about.

When we move further from medical matters, many of the crises in life are linked with people interacting – or not.

In business terms, it's referred to as 'interpersonal skills' and there are many training courses set up to address the associated concerns and problems. We will consider some of the problem areas – and criteria which can be used to approach some of the key sources and concerns – in later chapters.

Looking for the Best in People

One can't generalize about a whole species, but it is likely that many – perhaps even proportionately most of us – would act in an open, even altruistic way towards others to some extent, given that the perceived level of communication is open and non-threatening. We'll give a friend or family member a lift to an event or meeting without complaining. We'll try to help someone if they ask us for directions. We'll even lend a hand to tidy up at the end of a community event, where there may not be any people employed to do it.

The combined result of helping people like this gives emanations of love and happiness towards others, caused by increases in certain chemicals in our brains called endorphins. This all adds up to allowing us a more positive outlook to life, which also makes it easier for us to cope with and embrace any passing crises in life, should those nettles brush against our skin.

Example: Olympic Volunteers

This love application extends to volunteering. The 2012 London Olympics was a wonderful example of thousands upon thousands of people coming forward altruistically to offer their services, working long days and well into the night in many cases. There was the extra 'once in my lifetime' motivation of being involved in a unique lifetime event for their country but it still represented a monumental effort for these people. There was an atmosphere that grew rapidly ... a happy atmosphere. One might even call it a loving atmosphere around the various stadia and locations, one which emanated from spectators and participants alike. And even the press, after a few initial exposures of ticketing and security problems, were swept along on the tide of positivity.

One interesting outcome of all this positivity has been a heightened public comparison of this with the often egotistical – and increasingly unacceptable – way that some professional footballers conduct themselves. Perhaps through time, their value, both as role models for youngsters and in salary terms, will be gradually reappraised and the sport aspect of football may overshadow commercialism to a greater degree once again. Certainly, the short-term legacy of these 2012 London Olympics has been a wonderful example of positivity and individual creativity – let's hope that this can be extended into the longer term, for general co-operative interactions as well as in encouraging increased involvement in sport. We can certainly learn lessons in terms of working and living more harmoniously together, to reduce the incidence of those crisis nettles we may encounter.

Aquarian Changes

In moving into the age of Aquarius, we are undoubtedly experiencing great change. We are moving from the Piscean authoritarian and heavily structured stance to one of greater co-operation and openness – an atmosphere of love, in its widest sense. The role of women is changing, potentially creating a stronger shift towards peace and justice. The transition period will be long and complicated – and like all pendulum movements, there will be overreactions at both extremes before the equilibrium point is reached. For example, the involvement of women in jobs which were previously masculine domains leaves the male potentially feeling threatened at the same time as the female encounters a feeling of greater liberation and strength. In time, these over-compensations of the pendulum – those potential nettles of life (even at crisis proportions on occasion) will settle back, hopefully bringing a more relaxed, co-operative environment to the workplace – with improved personal interactions a certainty. In the intervening time, there may of course be periodic crises due to those aberrations.

The problems associated with this general shift from authoritarian to co-operative are also being played out in the turbulent ebbs and flows of what has been dubbed the 'Arab Spring'. It is being found that nations of people who have experienced a lifetime of authoritarian rule cannot necessarily slip easily into a co-operative, democratic role, where all voices expect to be heard equally. There will be many surges from side to side in society before acceptable equilibrium points are reached – this has to be expected. Effective communication strategies become very important, in order to meet the challenge of moving forward consistently.

Love in the Now

Positive progression is a long-term goal, moving from an egotistical state towards one of selfless altruism. It's a 'twisty' track but we should not be going down the 'what's in it for me?' route, as we look towards the future rather than the Now. Our attitudes will resolve in time, as things progress naturally through each Now moment. We're not bringing up our children so that they can look after us in our old age; we're not helping someone resolve a problem so that they 'owe us one' for the future. We're displaying love towards another or others simply because it's the right thing to do, at that moment, to allow us all to cope more easily.

Example: *What Goes Around, Comes Around*

I remember, as a teenager, going on a hillwalking holiday to the Cairngorms with my brother. We were travelling on a motorbike which, with two people and a load of camping and walking gear on board, was probably being stretched beyond its capabilities. On the rough roads around that area, the inevitable happened – we got a puncture in the back tyre. Mending this puncture involved removing the back wheel completely, which in those days also necessitated disconnecting the chain and rear brake.

We were struggling, when a passing motorist stopped and helped us complete the task – and when I say 'helped us', he in effect did it, with us supporting as best we could. Dealing with the dirty tyre and oily chain made a lot of mess, as you can imagine and we were pathetically grateful by the end of the process, wanting to thank him in some way.

I still remember him saying, 'You don't have to give me anything – just do the same for someone else in the future and that's reward enough'. That must have been over fifty years ago but the lesson still sticks in my mind and surfaces periodically when I spot someone needing assistance. I don't think I've helped an actual motorcyclist but jump-starting cars with dead batteries, helping to change car wheels and towing cars out of Scottish snow drifts are all in the same ball park!

Thus, we are approaching each positive act of love (or co-operation) towards another as it is happening in that Now moment. We ask ourselves what the need is and how we can respond to it – or indeed if there is someone present who can respond better (which may then revise what our offered action should be). I'm reminded of the story of an accident where a cyclist has fallen off his bicycle. A crowd has (inevitably) gathered and someone is bending over the injured cyclist. A new arrival pushes her way officiously through the crowd, shouting 'out of the way, out of the way – I'm a qualified First Aider at my workplace'. Pushing the person attending the cyclist to one side, she starts to go through the steps and stages she has learned on her training course. Finally, she hears a quiet voice at her side, from the person she has so roughly pushed aside. 'When you come to the point where your training says 'call for a doctor', just to say, I'm already here!'

Each of us has a role to play. Knowing our own strengths and shortfalls, however, will help each of us decide how best to help. (I prefer to use 'shortfall', indicating the possibility of learned improvement – whereas the more usual 'weakness' seems more negative). One of my shortfalls is with car engines, especially in these days of computerized fault diagnosis, so I don't offer to gaze at the engine of a disabled car as I'd have no idea what to do and might just uselessly raise the motorist's hopes. But I do know a fair bit about DIY, so would happily offer my services there. I am aware of my strengths and shortfalls even in this area, however. I'd thus happily defer to a tradesperson with honed skills – although I might still offer to hold things for him or her! However we elect to help, we are emanating positive love. Through these emanations, we are learning to cope – not by facing up to negative problems but by realizing our true potential and understanding – and then executing its best applications. We are, of course, also gaining better self-esteem – and through this, more self-confidence.

Gender Aspects to Grasping Nettles

Another interesting progression, which will take time to stabilize within decision-making in society as well as business, is the intrinsically different attitude towards problem-solving by men and women (as proposed in the Mars/Venus theory). If I can generalize, the feminine aspect leans towards sympathetic discussion and empathy with the person or people experiencing the problem, while the male tendency is towards offering solutions. We can doubtless all think of situations domestically as well as in our working environment where this basic difference has created relationship problems!

Notice, incidentally, that we are focused on aspects rather than gender. Men can display the feminine aspect to varying degrees (and *vice versa*, obviously), where they will respond to the feelings of the other party to a greater extent and hold back on providing cut-and-dried solutions. Similarly women may display less empathy towards their colleagues than might be expected. It all points towards complicated communications, presenting great scope for misinterpretation! But, as co-operation grows in line with a heightened awareness, some of the other 'love' synonyms we considered above, such as friendship, regard, respect and warmth, are likely to be applied more universally in general inter-relationships.

The Light of Love

As with the positive and the negative that we considered earlier, we have the light and the darkness. We live for the light. We look to the light but we are also aware of the darkness. Darkness need not be negative: the dark phases of our life, in daily terms, are necessary for rejuvenation, through sleep. Attempting to work in the hours of darkness proves problematic for many – we need the light. We need this energy from the sun, in order to maintain our positive outlook on life and personal interactions.

How do you regard this energy? Many would call it God, while others will say there is no God – yet most individuals will have their own vision of how they understand the concept. What works for you is right, especially if you've given due time and thought to considering it fairly deeply. My understanding is one of a universal Energy, with the power to create, evolve and even destroy selectively, if deemed necessary. Thinking more in energy or positive power terms, what do we have as the ultimate energy creator? We have the sun – the sun of God – which also provides us with the light – the positive loving light, generating and encouraging love in all its senses. We will be aware of SAD (Seasonal Affective Disorder) – also known as 'winter depression', which affects many people due to the lack of bright sunlight during winter months. We need this energy, be it from God or from the sun, in order to recharge our own personal batteries, relying on our own positives and negatives.

At a recent channelling I attended as a supporter/questioner, we requested a benediction which could be used by all as a mental and spiritual focus to apply before starting a meeting of minds of any type. This is what was given:

I am at peace with myself
And all surrounding me.
I am one with Love
And this flows through all things I am with.
I am Light.

'I am one with Love … I am Light'. We not only need light – through emanations of consciousness, of love but we also become light. Each of us is a glimmer of energy which, when combined together, generate light holistically … bringing an effect which is greater than the sum of the individual parts.

I was involved in an initiative to encourage people to think positively about peace at the start of the 2012 Olympics, at the precise moment when the flame was lit on the cauldron. As it turned out, the cauldron was designed as a beautiful, multi-flame installation, representing each of the countries attending, and was lit not by a single torchbearer but by seven athletes selected to represent the youthful hope of the future. This awesome sculpture, rising to create a final multiple flame, prolonged the moment beautifully, as around the world, thoughts of peace were focused during the activity. This focus was on light from hearts filled with positive love, helping to build hope and positive attitudes towards the future. In this, I believe it was successful.

Heartfelt Light and Darkness

We also periodically experience darkness in the mental and physical sense. This is a deeper subject. Using the same analogy as we did with daylight and night-time darkness, we could say that we need the experience of darkness in our lives to appreciate the positive, light-filled times which we enjoy … or have enjoyed. The problem is, perhaps, that there are occasions when we don't fully realize that life as we've known it was on the positive swing of the pendulum rather than 'normal'.

As people grow older, activities which they did without thinking become harder (or sometimes impossible) to do. This can be very frustrating (more so when younger people assume they can still perform as before!) but once again, thinking in the Now can help in readjusting to new circumstances. Alternatives can be identified, in order to maintain some response, albeit parallel. A potential crisis can thus be alleviated.

Example: Music with Arthritic Hands

I used to be actively involved as a folk singer, playing finger-style guitar to a reasonably proficient level and performing in concerts and folk clubs around Scotland in my late teens and twenties. In my mid-fifties, I began to experience arthritis in my hands, which gradually developed to the point at which I could no longer finger the chords properly. Casting my mind back to my successful past, it became immensely frustrating that I could not play in any of the Now moments when I might have picked up the guitar and played for my own enjoyment or to accompany singers. Thinking of the future – and the fact that I would never again be able to play the guitar properly – was also quite depressing.

But then I focused on the Now – what could I do to give wings to my musical creativity? Firstly, I discovered that my fingers worked better for four strings than six, so I bought a ukulele, which I can still play (although I find the sound less satisfying than the guitar … perhaps I'll have to practise more!). More importantly, my partner Jackie introduced me to the concept of improvized sound, using a range of instruments. We went on various courses and I started trawling eBay and specialist music stores to build up a wonderful collection of instruments from around the world.

We now provide soundings for meditation (which we call 'sound baths') using a varying range of instruments, as well as playing in concerts, peace events – and basically everywhere that will welcome improvized, inspirational sound.

So, from a position of creative darkness, light shines once again.

Converting Darkness to Light

Of course, I would be the first to acknowledge that there are dark experiences in life that are much harder to adjust to. As we've already discussed at some length, ongoing or terminal illnesses are an obvious example. On the plus side, I'm conscious of several people who have got through the dark side of a longterm illness by having it proved medically that they don't have cancer or some other dreaded disease. In other words, illness persists and nothing has been medically 'healed', other than the mental crisis or fear of what might be. The patient's concerns were dwelling on what darkness might evolve in the future rather than focusing on what was actually occurring in the Now. This is a deep psychological subject, which I wouldn't pretend to understand, other than to observe that, when the future-based fear element is addressed, the body is put in a stronger place to tackle its own self healing in the Now. 'The mind is its own place….'

And, even when the patient does have a potentially terminal illness such as cancer, his or her attitude towards it, focusing on what can be achieved in each 'Now' moment to make life as acceptable as possible, can make a world of difference. 'What interesting or exciting thing can I do today or next week to make my life as fulfilled as possible?' rather than 'I will feel worse in a month or so, so I'd better conserve my energy just now.' My personal view is that, in such circumstances, it is better to embrace as many nettles – and roses – as you can, even though you ultimately run out of energy and die slightly earlier, if the alternative is to retreat into a protective shell, experience little new and 'live' slightly longer. How do we equate 'living longer' anyway? Shine some light from new experiences into the darkness and enjoy it as you may. Having a belief in reincarnation can help as well!

Karmic Milestones

Let's think once more of each individual glimmer of light and how they build. I have written elsewhere in my two-book set of inspirational sayings (MESSAGES FROM THE MOUNTAINS and ECHOES IN THE ATRIUM) about visualizations relating to our pathway along the track of Life. I also apply this visualization in self-development workshops I have run periodically.

Let's try to practise it … though, as you're going to visualize this meditatively with your eyes closed, you'll have to get someone else to read it to you – or record it to play back! However it is presented to you, make sure it is spoken slowly, with plenty of pauses between paragraphs and even sentences, to give you a chance to take it all in.

Visualization: The Track of Life

Sit comfortably, close your eyes and concentrate on your breathing. Breathe slowly in and out, taking time to focus on what you are doing. Listen to the sound of your breath as it enters your nostrils and then as you exhale, through your slightly pursed lips. Gradually breathe more deeply and slowly, holding your breath for a few moments at the point when your lungs are comfortably full. You are concentrating totally on your breathing and not paying attention to any distracting sounds which might be going on around you. You are at peace.

Now I want you to imagine or visualize that you are out in the countryside. Around you, fields and woodland areas stretch off into the distance. The blue sky is dotted with beautiful, white, fluffy clouds, making all manner of shapes. Perhaps you can see the shape of a bird, an animal or an angel moving gracefully across the sky. You are standing at the start of a long straight track, which heads off into the distance.

This track presents the potential – the scope of possibilities that are available to each one of us. Notice that there are boundaries to this track. On either side, we have areas which make natural barriers, such as hedges of hawthorn, beech or briar; while, for other sections of the boundary, you can see man-made fences, some with barbed wire on top to make it even harder to cross. Occasionally, you may notice sections of brick or stone walls presenting a more solid barrier. Periodically, on either side, there are clumps of stinging nettles leaning out into the track, ready to sting you if your concentration fades or you are distracted.

Look around you – and ahead, down the track. Those

barriers are there to keep you progressing within known guidelines. But notice that, periodically, there are stiles built on the fences, to allow you to cross over if you choose. Notice also that, if you look closely, there are slight gaps in the hedges, which you could push through if you wished to see the options available on the far side of these barriers. There may even be an occasional gate. The choice is yours, knowing that you can always find another way to get back onto the main track again, if ambitious plans don't quite work out.

The man-made fences represent the constraints and parameters under which we exist. They are the rules and regulations, the restrictions, the laws and the financial or social limitations which influence our lives. The hedges represent the more natural criteria which colour our individual lives. These may be, for example, our personal beliefs, the standards which we have been brought up to observe and the pressures we might experience from our peers. These are all certainly guidelines, there to assist us but, on occasion, they may become inhibitors, potentially preventing us from using our own initiative or imagination. We will always continue to have some freedom of choice, regardless of the rules and parameters which abound. Take a moment to think about some of your key priorities and intentions … and how important they are to you. Bear in mind that there will always be some scope for thinking beyond the parameters – for exploring beyond the main boundaries of life … with care!

Pay special attention to the clumps of nettles. Some of these grow around the stiles, giving us some extra grief should we try to be more adventurous. Some will be growing deep in the hedgerows, ready to sting us if we try to push through. And some will be perfectly visible at the sides of the track – we can easily keep clear of these, as long as we keep our wits about us and concentrate on the way ahead. And remember, ultimately, that being stung might be painful for a minute or two but may well be worth the experience, to gain some new level that we want to achieve. Thinking in the Now, it may well be worth the short-term discomfort.

Now, I'd like you to focus your gaze on the track itself. If you look more closely, you may visualize regular milestones stretching away into the distance. These are the potential goals or objective checkpoints which are available to us, as individuals. Each of us will choose some of these goals – to form a sequence through which we will be progressing to establish our individual development. Some may have to be achieved before progressing to others; some may be realized in any sequence, when the opportunity arises, or the time is right. Obviously, many people will be pursuing the same or similar goals, so we may encounter bottlenecks periodically, if there are restrictions in timing, available teaching or equipment … or any of the other blockages which may present themselves.

Don't view these blockages negatively. Everything is intended, so they may be there to give you time to consolidate, reconsider priorities, review your future path forward …. or even to reassess whether an alternative path might be preferable. Consider each as a Now moment, where your pace of life can be reduced and your thoughts can be rationalized slowly and deeply. The renewed answer will present itself!

So, your individual path between your chosen milestones will not be a straight line – not by any manner of means! And then, of course, there will be lots of other individuals, each with his or her own sequence of goals.

Spend a moment thinking about your possible path – and about the other people you may encounter in your travels.

- *You may want to pause at this point – and meditate quietly for some time on the information and awareness which has come to you during this visualization.*
- *When you are ready, gradually bring yourself back to an awareness of your breathing and your surroundings. Once you've opened your eyes, make notes of any ideas or thoughts which have come to you.*
- *As a subsequent visualization exercise, you may wish to listen to the first section once more but this time continue straight into the second section, which follows.*

Visualization – Part Two

Imagine for a moment that you can fly. It's easy really, if you focus!

Visualize that you are flying high above the track, as high as a skylark, so that you can look down on the track stretching both ahead and into the past. Remember that you are a spark of energy – that each of us is a glowing light. You will see a myriad of these twinkling sparks along the path below you, with trails of light indicating the individual paths being followed. You may see your own personal glow of energy – clearer because of your personal link with it.

See how you have progressed – at times in almost straight lines; at other times looping around like illuminated spaghetti! You will see where your progress has been crossed by the paths of others – or where several paths have converged on the same milestone, waiting for availability of people or resources. You may also see where you've had to double back, on occasion, to complete a goal which was outstanding, at an earlier point in your path. And bear in mind that each of these other sparks of energy represented on the path is an individual – a colleague or partner, new or old – moving along his or her path of development and enlightenment.

Look to left and right of the boundaries and you will see how some lights have taken the initiative and experimented on the far outreaches of the track. Some individuals have got stuck, some have meandered for a while before returning to the track – while a few lights are progressing in a straight line in the outer reaches, uninhibited by the majority. All ways are possible, if the situation and attitudes are right.

Always remember that it's important to keep the 'big picture' in mind. Here's another situation where you have to think in the Now – but have also to bear the past and future in mind. You'll evidently be aware of your progress to date – and have ideas of the future goals you have established for your personal development and enlightenment path. But this future path must be reviewed objectively, step by step in each Now moment, to maintain progress and respond to any changing priorities.

At times, these changes may be imposed by others – and may therefore be hard to accept. At work, goalposts may be shifted, making some of the effort you've put into doing things immediately obsolete. This is difficult to swallow, but the sooner you can reposition and get ready for positive progress once more, the better it will be for your personal development.

Now, to end this visualization, take a moment focusing on your own glimmer of light and the path that it has taken so far. Look to the future and clarify in your mind what some of your own key future goals may be. Thinking in the Now, establish what your next immediate goal should be – and how you might best achieve this. What will your personal strategy be? Who might you have to call upon, to assist you?

Take a few moments to consider this, then focus on your breathing once more – and when you feel grounded again, open your eyes and rest for a few minutes.

You may find it helpful to make some notes about your past progress and any requirements necessary to make these future plans a reality.

Thank you.

Conclusion

So, love in all its many facets is both foundation and building block of the structure which we call life. Thinking and acting altruistically or selflessly is a strong step along our way to positive personal development and enlightenment, built on the foundations of respect, co-operation, attentiveness and awareness of the feelings of others.

Thinking in terms of energy, we relate the positive energy of the individual with the healing and growing energy of the sun. Spiritually, if that is the language we choose, this would be considered as the fundamental God Energy, which is the creator and regenerator of all things. Applying these principles positively and grasping the nettles which can stand in our way and restrict progress, we can review our path objectively and progressively, amending specifics as necessary to maintain growth.

Meditative Thought

This poem links with the visualization, where we were
considering the response at each Now moment, when the
'goalposts had shifted' slightly and we needed to review
our options and the probable way forward. It encourages
an open, loving overview of the 'bigger picture', in order
to keep us thinking positively and moving onwards towards
the light of enlightenment.

Don't Mistake the Weather for the Sky

When things are not quite going as intended
And you can't understand the reason why,
Then spend a while, just linking with your soul now
And don't mistake the weather for the sky.

There's phases when you almost lose direction
However hard you think, or hard you try,
They're there to make you focus on your values,
When you've mistaken weather for the sky.

It's often other folks who cause the problems
But not in any bad or selfish way -
It's just your thoughts and actions have to fit in
With those of others, dealing day to day.

You may have plans, ambitions or intentions,
Though obstacles can come, to make you cry –
But don't, just take a while to reposition
And not mistake the weather for the sky.

The weather's often grey with clouds foreboding;
There's rain and snow, winds fit to snap a rope;
While sky is all around, a welcome mantle
With sun or stars, it's there to give us hope.

So, when those blocks appear and you're
    downhearted,
First scan the sky for inspiration new;
Seek out the loving ways to restart progress –
Alternatives, that you can follow through.

And when you move once more, in new direction –
Enlightened now to reach new values high –
You'll then forget the problems you encountered
When you mistook the weather for the sky.

Chris Sangster

CHAPTER SIX

THE POWER OF SOUND

THERE IS no doubt that music or sound can have a therapeutic or soothing effect. Music – and sounding too – both have a strongly healing effect on many people, helping them to cope with stress. Recorded and live music, singing singly or in groups, even humming to yourself in the bath, all can play a part in healing strategies. Doing voicework or playing instruments in groups brings us together through what is referred to as entrainment. This, basically, is the phenomenon by which people interacting musically will gradually drift so that they are ultimately toning in harmony with each other – or playing the same or complementary rhythms. This has positive effects in building teams at work, or encouraging people to feel safer in a crowd.

It is also very evident that music and sound have different effects on different people. I personally find the music of Aeoliah and Steven Halpern very relaxing and appropriate for both meditation and healing. Others consider it to be too 'electronic' – or refer to such electronic sounds as being 'crematorium music'! With the group I attend in Wiltshire, our favourite piece for entering an altered state for channelling is Wagner's Prelude to the first act of his opera *Lohengrin* – we consider it blissful, while some people find Wagner generally rather overwhelming. The list of contrasts could go on.

The same is true for using sound improvization instruments in healing, meditation and generally when helping people relax and cope. One either loves or hates the didgeridoo and some people become unsettled by the persistent sound of African *djembe* drumming – while others really get deeply into the rhythm. Fairly evidently, from a sound therapy point of view, the 'patient' has to feel an affinity with each instrument being used, for positive effect. For single instrument therapists, this is perhaps inbuilt. For example, one would assume that if a patient didn't feel comfortable with the sounds of gongs, he or she wouldn't seek out a gong therapist. As we use a range of instruments in our work, we have to spend some time establishing those which have the desired positive effect – and those which are best to set aside for that particular session or participant.

How Healing Works

This simple formula, SOUND + INTENTION = HEALING, attributed to American sound healer Jonathan Goldman, is often quoted as the way sound healing operates successfully. Put simply, if I strike a gong with the heartfelt intention that the resultant sound will cause healing in my patient, then healing will result. Put slightly egotistically, because I believe my created sound has a healing property, then some healing and coping effect is likely to result.

As you're probably aware, there's a vast variety of relaxation and 'spiritual' music on the market, from the truly sublime to the extremely mundane. As I've mentioned earlier, music which one person identifies as being soul shifting could really grate with another listener. We must therefore carefully select the instruments used during a sound healing or meditation session. Similarly, specific artists, instruments and tracks on CDs must be identified carefully, to allow the intention to transmit properly – to be absorbed or received positively by the patient or participant.

It is said that the power of intention involves consciously drawing down spiritual energy, in the same way that healing energy can pass through the hands of the en-tuned masseur. Thus, what I propose we need to add to the equation is the positive awareness of the patient receiving this energy, which would give us the extended formula :

$$SOUND + INTENTION + RECEPTION = HEALING$$

Choice of Instruments

Instruments which we would tend to suggest for selection for sound healing would come from the following list.

Shamanic drum,
   Flute,
      Tibetan singing bowls,
        Chinese gongs,
         Glockenspiel,
          Freenotes,
           Table tubes.

Freenotes are a form of very precise metal xylophone. I'd add various secondary percussion instruments for variety.

If the particular instrument or instruments has/have been first discussed and identified, the therapist can focus on the intention, in the knowledge that the reception is as open and positive as can be expected. It is thus more likely that the inspired energy can flow through one to the other, with some degree of healing outcome more likely. The stronger the intention (and belief that a transfer of healing energy will happen), the greater and more positive the end-result can be.

Sound therapy is the act of identifying sound vibrations which are lacking or deficient in the patient and augmenting these through soundings, using specific instruments. As we have previously identified, the close vibrations from a shamanic drum or gong, or the soothing notes from a flute or metalphone, can have a therapeutic effect on the receptive patient. Similar effects can of course be achieved using pre-recorded music. Through the ages, music and sound have had a very powerful effect in helping people cope with stress, pain and even fear.

Choice of Music

We've already established that choice of music is a subjective process, but it may be valuable to identify my selection of ten CDs which I would choose to take to the proverbial desert island. They're listed in no particular order but each one has tracks which I can listen to, over and over again. Some are great for meditation and healing sessions, while others are good for stilling and relaxing the mind, or even just using as background music. I actually found it very difficult to limit the choice to ten, so these really *are* the 'cream of the crop' for me.

TITLE	ARTIST	LABEL
Angel Love	Aeoliah	Oreade Music
Majesty	Aeoliah	Oreade Music
Chill Out Mantras	Various	Global Journey
Password	Deva Premal	Sounds True
Deep Theta	Steven Halpern	Inner Peace Music
State of Grace	Paul Schwartz	Windham Hill
Music for Healing	Stephen Rhodes	New World Music
Canyon Trilogy	R Carlos Nakai	Canyon Records
Soul Storm	Tim Wheater	Imagemaker
Classical Chillout	Various	EMI & others

I'd further recommend any Russian male voice choir singing spiritual music. We were honoured to come across four
members of the 'Doros' male vocal ensemble singing in the
cathedral at Carcassonne, during a visit to Cathar country in
southern France in 2012. Their close-harmony singing in the
acoustically-charged cathedral was absolutely face-tingling!

Entrainment

As I mentioned in the opening paragraphs, the combination of intention and reception creates a bond which can
be recognized and developed within groups of participants.
It's generally considered that we all have our 'natural note' –
the note that we vibrate to and which we will individually
sing naturally. Linking with this, when we sing or sound
together, interesting effects develop. Here's something to try.

Exercise: Group Sounding

Gather together a group of friends and form a circle. If you really want to bond, link arms round necks at shoulder level and lean slightly in towards the centre of the circle. The purpose of the exercise is for each individual to sound his or her own note at the same time and to keep sounding (and breathing between soundings of your note!) for an extended period of time. There are no rules, other than to maintain the sounding.

What you should find is that, even though the initial sound consists of a wide range of individual notes, a group sound will gradually evolve. There may be a bit of a 'power struggle' in the early stages, where individuals are striving to maintain their individual notes, but gradually a specific note will always evolve. This could initially be because it's close to the notes of several individuals – or it could be because one sounder has a more powerful voice, or sounds more confidently.

The next stage is the magical one! Once the generalized group note has been reached, ego struggles cease and everyone concentrates on listening to and maintaining the note. Because of the tonal range of the voices, some will find it easier to sing in harmony, so harmonies will gradually evolve. Some of the more adventurous will start to vocalize between the harmonies, creating little glissandos between the harmonics, with the overall effect becoming quite blissful. Carry on for as long as you can.

This is the action of entrainment. A parallel effect can be achieved with a group using African *djembe* drums, where a rhythm gradually evolves from tentative beginnings, until they create an inspiring, precise beat, echoing around the hall or open space. Just as the voice soundings produced harmony, cross-rhythms will evolve naturally. In technical terminology, entrainment is defined as the mutual phase-locking of different oscillators.

In sound terms, it's where the group's actions merge holistically, to some extent, to create a unified sound and/ or tempo. This can have a strongly therapeutic, bonding effect on groups of people sounding together – sounding and drumming are both entrainment exercises which I have used in sound team-development events, thereby resolving conflict and building cohesion.

Altering Brain Wave States through Sound

At another level, entrainment happens when brain waves are influenced by a sound, which brings the brain to a different vibration, relating closely to the sound. We have a variety of brain-wave states, mainly incorporating Beta, Alpha, Theta and Delta, with Theta being the state of deep meditation. The vibration necessary for this altered state to be entrained is generally considered to be in the region of 6 Hertz (Hz). This can be created in hand-tuned, cast or beaten instruments, where two notes which have this fractional difference are sounded together. As an example, the A above middle C on the piano has a vibration of 440 Hz. If we have two A notes being sounded on gongs, where one is at 440 Hz while the other is in reality 446 Hz, the lesser will cancel out the 440 in the second higher one, leaving the difference (6 Hz) to entrain the brain wave to Theta wavelengths over time.

A very good double CD which both explains and illustrates these effects is *Self Healing with Sound and Music* by Dr Andrew Weil and Kimba Arem, produced by Sounds True. Steven Halpern has also produced a series of CDs where the music and soundings are created to induce these particular brain-wave states (if used carefully in the correct conditions).

Good Sound : Bad Sound

At this point in our considerations of sound within a coping context, we should perhaps give some thought to more negative sounds. Life, as we know, is not all relaxation and singing bowls, so we must face up to the stresses and strains caused by negative or intrusive sound.

Most of us are exposed to some extent to loud or sudden noise. Even when my wife and I lived up in the remote west coast of Scotland, the silence of our walks in the fields (with only an occasional sheep bleating, dog barking or buzzard calling on the wing for company) was periodically rudely interrupted by the sudden scream of RAF fighter jets using our local loch for low-level flight training.

In a more urban existence, we may have experienced the souped-up Fiesta with purple lights flashing underneath, head-banging occupants and a staccato, massively-amplified beat drilling the road and probably rearranging internal organs!

With much of modern pop music which has a solid beat, a particular rhythm is referred to as the 'stopped-anapaestic' rhythm (beats of short, short, long, pause) which, as well as distressing the bodily heart rhythms, also (amazingly) has the effect of weakening the listener's muscles. Then there are all the 'background' sounds of road works, traffic, trains and aircraft flying overhead or (worse still) landing. These are all examples of sound or noise which can have a strongly detrimental effect on us, certainly causing stress over time – and occasionally reaching crisis proportions, when we begin to feel powerless.

Now: How to Cope?

We can attempt to cope with obtrusive, negative sound in a variety of ways. Many of these involve isolating ourselves from excessive noise as much as possible. We can always leave the room if there is too much noise or loud music playing – or use ear plugs to limit the entry of the noise to our eardrums. We could also consider using noise-cancelling headphones, which rather cleverly negate the extraneous noises around us, again using the technique of entrainment, allowing quieter levels of music-listening on the 'phones.

I'm usually surprised when I switch on the car engine in the drive and the radio/CD player comes on, playing at the volume I was listening on the way home the previous day. In the relative peace of a static vehicle in the drive, it seems very loud – but this is the volume we would normally have while driving, to be heard above the engine and road noise (otherwise referred to as the ambient noise). Again, think of that if you drive a lot with the radio/CD player on.

Noise Protection

Thus, generally speaking, coping with negative or loud noise involves attempting to isolate yourself from it as much as possible. If you can remove yourself from the situation, do so. Otherwise, wear ear protection of some description. Health and Safety at work dictates that hearing protection is worn in noisy environments. Many older people suffer from poor hearing now because these precautions were not in force when they were at work. Nothing can totally protect ears from heavy artillery fire, so many soldiers (and civilians caught up in the fighting) will suffer from some ear damage – as indeed is still being experienced by some former conscripts from the Second World War. Sixty-plus years of background tinnitus is a lot to cope with!

Using the Voice

We all have a voice, which we can use to a greater or lesser extent for singing. Having said that, at the point when I entered hospital with severe throat problems, the guy in the next bed was being discharged, having had parts of his larynx removed which prevented him from speaking, let alone singing. That required me to focus very much on the Now rather than the future, to maintain a positive take on my own future position!

At some level, most of us can gain some degree of relaxation through singing or using the voice. Some of us may have been prevented from singing in the school choir – or even been told to keep quiet at home! – but there are many ways and levels at which we can operate in the quest to express ourselves positively.

Singing, singly or in groups, is certainly a stress-release mechanism – singing in the bath or shower has been around since plumbing was invented! Actually singing along to music, rather than merely listening to the song, also gives a heightened effect. I have a mantrabox, which is a small plastic box some 7 x 5 x 2 cms in size, with digitally pre-recorded 'loops' containing a range of mantra chants. I played this quietly on many occasions while in hospital (when in a side single room, I hasten to add – the other patients wouldn't have appreciated it while I was in the main wards!) I found that its effectiveness was on a sliding scale: quite effective when I was just listening to it; more effective if I was concentrating on the words that were being said (even though I didn't understand what they meant); most effective, by a wide margin, when I actually sang along with it. This, I believe, was largely on account of having to focus on singing in time with the recorded chant – as well as developing the concentration necessary to maintain the chant over an extended period of time.

Toning a chant over an extended period of time in this way gives us a focus, at the same time as cutting out any extraneous thoughts and sounds which could otherwise be a distraction (as they might be, for example, during a silent meditation). Group chanting in this way is another application of entrainment and certainly allows release of stress by eliminating distracting thoughts and giving us a focus which helps with overall balance.

Exercise: Overtoning

Here's something new in sound which you may not have experienced before. There's a particular type of chanting – created, I believe, by Tibetan monks – which is called overtoning. With this, as well as having the fixed tone as a bass foundation, movement of the mouth and tongue create related harmonics which sound simultaneously. If you call up

'Overtoning *Amazing Grace*' on YouTube, you will find many examples of videos where people are chanting a note, while picking out the tune of the hymn *Amazing Grace* using the harmonics. Look out for one by Nestor Kornblum, who is particularly talented! Once you get the idea of how over-toning should sound, give it a try. It basically sounds like a quiet whistling of different notes in the background, with the basic sound acting like a continuous drone. Move your lips and tongue around while toning and, sooner or later, you will produce an overtone. *Amazing Grace* may elude you in your early stages of exploration but try to get a few different harmonics sounding. It's very satisfying!

Summary: a Range of Benefits

To sum up, music and sound can help us cope with personal crises in a range of different ways. As patient or recipient, we can gain therapeutic and healing benefits from sound baths and treatments using selected instrument sounds.

Ambient music can be used in relaxation and also more specifically to entrain particular wave patterns in the brain to aid meditation and relaxation. Indirectly, of course, this encourages a better state of mind to think logically and problem-solve more effectively.

And, thirdly, personal involvement in the uses of sound, through playing, singing, chanting and any other way of focusing on expressing ourselves, can have a major effect on our ability to cope with some of the nettles of life. The concentration, relaxation and satisfaction involved in the applications of sound in these ways help us to address concerns to a heightened degree.

Meditative Thought – Fading to Stillness

Silence and sound are the *yin* and *yang* of life – the energy-directed light and dark which make us aware of opposites and draw our attention to the inner stillness through which we can communicate with higher energies through meditation. When we can push aside the apparent need for constant external stimulation and link with the stillness within, only then will we be truly at one. The applications of sound through indigenous instruments use silence as well as sound – the sound decay of the gong or bowl and the silence it becomes is as soul-stimulating as the initial note when the beater strikes.

The poem on the next two pages approaches sound from this different angle – from the over-riding silence of an early morning in Stenness, in Orkney. We were there as a group to visit spiritual sites and our temporary home stood alone on a promontory near the Ring of Brodgar (one of the largest Neolithic stone circles in the United Kingdom). In such a situation, when waking in the early morning, my immediate awareness was of absolute silence. Then, gradually, I heard the natural sounds around, with each as fresh as spring grass – becoming acutely aware that silence is also a sound, to nurture and protect us and help us cope.

Waking up at Stenness

Listen to the silence
As it calls around your head;
The creaks, the bird-calls, lamb-bleats
In a landscape seeming dead.

Hear the latent energy
As it crackles in the air,
Drowned by car, then birdsong,
Or footstep on the stair

Hear the sound of humans
As they slumber in the house;
The cough, the snore: that movement –
Was it human, maybe mouse?

Single bleat, persistent:
A lamb has lost its ewe,
Rushes hither, thither
Till mum comes back in view

Oystercatcher calls now;
Crows and hawks reply:
Ewe makes throaty rumbles
To summon lambs to try

To pump her flanks for succour,
To fill their bellies warm –

Then off for silent gambols
In groups, so safe from harm.

Gazing out the window
At loch and sea and stream –
No wind to ruffle surface
The views are like a dream.

Mute swans sail the surface
Silent and serene;
Standing stones watch voiceless
O'er this wondrous scene.

Waking up at Stenness,
Gazing o'er the stones,
Lost in dreams of ancients:
Why must we go home?

Chris Sangster

CHAPTER SEVEN

COMMUNICATING FOR NOW

A LARGE percentage of my involvement while I was a business training consultant encompassed communication – so I may be slightly biased! However, I would propose that many of the problems in business – and in life generally – with which we need to cope, are attributable to poor communication. Just think of a few examples – I would imagine you've had direct experience of some of these :

- strong assertion, moving over into aggression, in the way managers and colleagues/friends act towards you
- inappropriate statements being made about you, either to your face or behind your back
- incomplete information or directions being given to you, which often prolong the time required to complete a task correctly
- inconsiderate choice of written wording, which causes misunderstandings and offence
- information being provided to you, that doesn't take account of your level of awareness or knowledge about the subject.

You'll notice that many of these examples are not purely communication problems – they will tend to impact on how you can complete tasks, manage your time or relate to others, for example. Communication is the sound and vision which allows us to get the message across effectively … or not. You will also notice that the examples are all written to make you the 'poor me' recipient of deficient (or downright bad) communication. Hand on heart – have you ever been the giver rather than the receiver? Each of these situations will cause stress and other problems to some degree. Each of these will need a coping strategy – or, thinking positively, an alternative strategy to improve the joint communication in the first place.

In this and subsequent chapters, we'll be referring to some of the 'best practice' ways of doing things, which are taught in business training workshops. I will be trying to 'translate' these so that they're equally useful in our day-to-day life. For both the work and life aspects of our work–life balance, the application of these 'best practice' strategies will help us not only to cope better – but to avoid some of the stress-educing pitfalls in the first place! Occasionally, I'll have to use business jargon – but I'll try to keep it to a minimum, I promise!

Example: the Brewing Argument

Imagine the situation where someone says something to you in an aggressive way. There is a saying 'it takes two to make a fight'. How you respond will have a strong bearing on the remainder of that communication experience. There are several possibilities:

- *You could, of course reply equally aggressively. With some blustering bullies, this may have the desired effect, as they will back off rapidly. With those who are genuinely aggressive, however, your response is likely to escalate matters into a shouting match. The judgment of* whether they are blustering or genuine is one you have to make!

- You could agree with their stance or view, if you do largely agree with it or if you don't strongly care either way. This usually 'wrong-foots' the aggressor, who is unsure how to proceed, as he or she was expecting an argument.

- You could pause to compose yourself, then ask the aggressor why they feel so strongly about the matter (or words to that effect). You are shifting the focus from the facts to the delivery, inviting reasons to allow you to select the best way forward for the discussion.

- You could treat it as a joke. This is, of course, a risky strategy but it's flagging the fact that you don't consider the situation to be serious enough for aggression. If this strategy doesn't work, you always have the 'only joking' let-out clause – but as above, the judgment regarding the person's sense of humour is up to you!

- You could say nothing or walk away. It relieves the tension of the moment – but postpones the problem rather than resolves it. Many of us will have rushed out of the room during an argument (slamming the door is the real moment of satisfaction!) – but it does create the problem that you have to re-enter the room, actually or figuratively, at some future point, to resolve the issue.

There are doubtless other strategies that you can identify – spend a few moments thinking about them – but the important point here is that these are all potential actions that you, the receiver of the aggression, can take to change a negative situation into a more positive one.

Of course, the other side of the coin from a training perspective is that the aggressor can be trained (or monitored) to be more mindful about what he or she is saying and how it is being said (or written). There has been a massive shift in the last thirty years or so regarding what and how people can communicate in business, with internal warning systems, tribunals and even 'outings' in the press there to enforce improvement overall. Overall, progress is occurring.

Spoken Communications

In an earlier chapter, we considered the applications of love in dealing with each other and established the principle of 'doing as you would be done by'. As with a lot of wisdom, it's all very straightforward. Imagine that you are in a radio studio handling phone calls from the public. What precautions would you incorporate, to prevent someone saying inappropriate things live on air? You have a recording loop to allow a delay of several seconds between the caller speaking and the words being broadcast, allowing the plug to be pulled rapidly on 'Mr Abusive from Aberystwyth'. You, equally, can build in a 'love loop' into your communications, pausing for a moment to consider the effects of your statements before making them. It often helps to 'engage the brain before opening the mouth'!

Example: the Meaning of Words

Let's think about the effects of words for a moment. Studying a thesaurus periodically is a good exercise in becoming more aware of degrees of meaning. Take the verb 'ask', for example. My *Chambers Thesaurus* gives the following options, among others :

Appeal, apply, beg, beseech, crave, demand, implore, inquire, interrogate, invite, order, petition, plead, query, question, quiz, request, require, seek, solicit *and* summon.

Think of the range and degrees of meaning in the different words – and the various effects they would have on the receiver. Consider the following sentence :

'I ask you to give me help in resolving this problem.'

Now, replace 'ask' with – 'beg'; 'beseech'; 'demand that'; 'invite'; 'order'; 'request'; 'require' – and see the difference of degrees involved. Think about the effect of each.

At one extreme, we have 'beseech' and 'request', while at the opposite, we have 'order' and 'demand that'. Imagine your different reactions, if you were the receiver!

Also notice that some words given in the thesaurus are not appropriate for particular meanings. 'Interrogate' or 'quiz', for example, do involve asking but in more of a testing than a requesting way, so wouldn't be appropriate in this sentence. Using words in the wrong context is one of the pitfalls of using a thesaurus – if you don't understand the meaning of the word, check in the dictionary or use an alternative. There are invariably many to choose from.

Getting the Message Across

When you're communicating with others, you must remain consciously aware of how your message is being received – that's a crucial element of effective communication – and react to your awareness. If the listener's looking puzzled, you might have to explain things in greater detail or in simpler language. If the listener's looking annoyed, you may have to rapidly review what you've said, to identify where the problem lies … and do something to rectify the situation!

In the communication business, so to speak, the receivers are referred to as your 'target population'. It may sound a bit cold and technical but thinking about it like that does help you realize that you're actually aiming your language

or communication at a person or people. It's that love awareness again, in a communicative sense. Remain aware of your
audience and remember – there's more to communication
than immediately meets the eye!

Coping with the Fear of Public Speaking

In my business training days, some large percentage of the
courses I ran were on presentation skills, focusing on getting
a structured message across both verbally and through the use
of visual aids. Many of us may be involved in some form of
speaking in public, from talking to a few colleagues through
(potentially) to a full-blown auditorium presentation.

Giving any form of speech in public makes a lot of people feel very nervous. We're embracing major nettles here
– and will tackle the effects in greater detail in chapter nine.
The main nettle is probably fear.

What may we be afraid of? It might be the fear of drying
up – of forgetting what we were planning to say. Or it may
be of standing there with a vast sea of faces looking at you
(as you imagine it, willing you to make a mistake so that
they can laugh at you)! This is rarely the case, in reality –
and making and acknowledging a mistake in your speech
is often the moment when you strike an accord with your
audience!

In the film, *The Best Exotic Marigold Hotel*, Judi Dench's char-
acter is advised to think of her audience as being naked,
before giving her first presentation in the Indian call centre. Personally, I might find that rather distracting but if it
works for you…! I've rarely experienced a malicious audience (apart from a few secondary schools) and would say

that, if you can get the message at the correct level for your target population of adults, they will listen at least politely but more likely, with genuine interest.

Now, to the question of drying up. If you have your visual prompts, on the screen or as cards or paper in your hand or lectern, this really shouldn't be a problem. If you're using cards or paper, the principle of using key points applies. Think coat pegs to hang your ideas on – a brief word or phrase (written or printed *large*) will remind you of the detail which you want to elaborate further. If there are particular facts or figures which you need to quote (and which you're not confident of remembering), write them down on your prompt. It's there to give you confidence – you may not even need to refer to it when you're up there performing but, psychologically, you know you've got the support.

If your fear is one of speaking to large numbers of people, seek a lower-level opportunity to try out your skills or observe closely how others do it, to find out which techniques succeed (and which don't). For example, if you're not very good at telling jokes normally, don't even think of starting off your presentation with a joke – it and you are likely to fall flat! When you're up there, you won't usually be strongly aware of individual people anyway, other than those in the first two or three rows. So, initially, think of them as a general mass of bodies, rather than individuals.

Less Formal Presentations

Having spent years training people to follow these fairly structured and businesslike guidelines, I initially found it strange when I attended talks on more erudite, spiritual matters – which tended to be less formal. Many of the speakers didn't use any visuals or notes and just seemed to be speaking from the heart. There might be periodic long pauses, with the speaker thinking deeply (presumably) about what to say and the audience politely sitting waiting for the next pearl of wisdom. Others seemed to be very happy for members of the audience to interrupt with questions or rambling statements regarding their own experiences. Initially, I felt rather uncomfortable and dissatisfied because I was judging them in the 'old ways'. But gradually, I came to realize that they were, indeed, talking from the heart rather than the mind and that the overall effect was rather liberating.

It has to be said, I suppose, that these presentations do not have any of the reviews, assessments and other critical evaluations which have progressively constricted business training and presentations – and are all the more flexible and potentially vibrant because of this. For whatever reason, I found myself warming more and more to this fluid and honest style of presenting, while retaining one or two of the principles which I had drilled into hundreds if not thousands of delegates over the years. So, in the light of these revelations, here is my new, liberated message!

Example: Coping with Giving Presentations

Key tips:

- *Plan out a sequence of subject points you want to cover*
- *Write these as a brief bullet-point reference, for use before or during the talk*
- *Equate the content with the amount of time you're allowed (or need)*

- Break down your talk into 'digestible chunks', with pauses to rest the mind
- Get some idea of your expected audience levels and any special needs
- Arrange for any visual aids (pictures, books, models etc) you might need
- Decide whether you're going to stand or sit (or vary, using both)
- Check how loudly you have to speak to be heard (louder when the hall's full of people)
- Decide how you'll handle questions – during or at the end of the session – and tell your audience
- Keep checking on your sequence of main points and don't digress too much
- Keep an eye on the time – don't over-run. Finishing slightly early is not a problem.

Taking a tip from several 'spiritually-aware' presentations I've experienced, be reassured that if the session is running out of things for you to say and the question session isn't flowing, you can always finish with a meditation or a long pause for reflection!

So much for spoken communication. Basically, if we can cope with giving some form of more organized presentation, we should be more confident about coping with other, lesser forms of speaking. These could include proposing something at a meeting or developing a discussion about a topic when with colleagues – or even communicating your ideas successfully during those rambling discussions at the pub!

Writing as Catharsis

We can perhaps feel confident enough to use writing as a stress-release or coping mechanism, to combat anger or

grief, for example. In written communications skills training courses, I used to refer to writing the 'mantelpiece letter'. This was the letter which you wrote to the Managing
Director of a company that had messed you around, the
Editor of a newspaper – or to any other authoritative figure
you could identify. And why 'mantelpiece'? Because, having
written it, you put it on the mantelpiece overnight, rather
than rushing out and posting it.

The next morning, in the cooler heat of reason, you
could review the content, in order to decide whether you
still wanted to send it. Often, merely writing the letter had
got the anger out of your system, so you could 'post' it in
the bin; on other occasions, you might decide to revise
and rewrite the content before still sending it off – and of
course, on certain occasions, you would still decide to send
the letter as originally composed. You had, however, built
in a control loop – which might save you problems later,
where trying to defend a stance in which you perhaps now
only partially believed! The same principle can – and should
– be used when writing and sending contentious emails
and texts.

Some of us use creative writing as a form of catharsis as
well, to release grief, stress or even anger. While writing this
manuscript, my much-loved border collie, Star, who I've
mentioned several times within the text, deteriorated fast
with joint and breathing problems, to the extent that we
had to reach the decision (aided by her) to have her put to
sleep. It all happened very gently and peacefully but I woke
up in the middle of the night afterwards, full of grief but
unable to cry properly (I am a bloke, after all!)

With a mug of tea for company, I wrote the following
poem:

Star – 29/11/12

A full moon tonight,
And another Star has reached the sky.
True friend and companion,
We'd walked the land together
Many years.

The eyes said it:
Aches and problems turned to pain –
No longer comfort,
Uneasy pacing, panting breaths –
'Help me on'.

Turn the clock back.
Moving sheep and walking miles,
Kept on going;
Stamina and strength of will,
Loved companion.

Lying still now:
Heaving sides are calm at last.
Thoughts flow inward;
Flickering eyelids, final breath:
Goodbye dear friend.

Chris Sangster

It helped me come to terms with my grief – although I haven't managed to read it in public yet. Subsequently, I wrote a more extended poem, which I include at the end of this chapter (this one, I did – just – manage to read at my local poetry club). As you will perhaps note, it was intended to present a cheerier, more commemorative note but the latent grief still surfaces in the latter verses.

Writing down your thoughts – in any poetry or prose format – is generally thought to be a very good way of dealing with the milder levels of stress or trauma. Evidently, for more serious cases of trauma, specialist help should be sought. As with the 'mantelpiece letter' mentioned above, the writing down of the thoughts and emotions is very often more important than what happens to the document afterwards. In these cases, spelling and punctuation can be considered to be of lesser importance! The important thing is to express the emotions as openly and extensively as possible.

Coping with Written Communications

In terms of possibly creating stressful outcomes, we should perhaps briefly consider some of the special issues associated with written communications, including standards in written communication. With a little thought, you'll be able to subdivide your written communications into different levels of importance, with regard to the effort you put into having them accurate and well presented.

Many of your emails (especially those for business purposes) and any letters you still write, should be considered as potentially legal-level reference documents. Ask yourself whether any specific piece of writing could be used as written evidence at one level or another. Spending the time checking through what you've written and the wider interpretations and implications may save you having to establish coping strategies later, if or when your communication has created problems! While bearing in mind the accuracy of your missive, also spare a thought to the degree of friendly, open communication which you can inject into it. Picture the person when you're writing the words to them and keep asking yourself – 'how are these words going to affect them – and are they creating the atmosphere and effect I intend?'

As with many of the strategy considerations we've been reviewing latterly, there's a distinct case of 'prevention rather than cure'. Thinking through the possible effects and outcomes of an action before committing yourself to it – and applying some of the 'best practice' criteria we're covering – will help greatly in limiting the number of scenarios you'll find yourself in, which would otherwise have created stress and coping needs. Prevention, through conscious and unselfish thought and planning, is as much of a coping strategy as dealing with fallout after the crisis-ridden event!

If you're conscious of having difficulties with grammar, sentence construction and vocabulary, seek help. This could be by getting someone who is proficient to check your written documents – especially the important ones. If your range of vocabulary needs expanding, I suggest you invest in a thesaurus, which provides you with a good choice of words to avoid repetition.

Conclusion

In considering communication, we've been viewing it both from the 'best practice' stance of striving to get it right so that we avoid creating stressful problem situations – and from the aspect of using writing creatively and expressively to release tension. Using the structure and strategies for giving a presentation, we've seen how we can generally work at getting our messages across more clearly and 'humanly' – creating the effect that we intend.

Communicating through Poetry

Much of my poetry is written in response to particular emotions, experiences or images and to act as a catharsis for both capturing these feelings in a more permanent form and allowing them to release and flourish in a positive manner.

Meditative Thought

As mentioned above, I wrote the poem on the next two pages, in memory of my much-loved companion Star, who died in late 2012, at a slightly later point than the one on p. 127. Writing it (and reading it subsequently) continues to help me to cope with the great loss.

In Memory

I see you now – out on the hill:
We watched the flock together
As down we moved them, through the gate
No matter what the weather.

You came to me as puppy small –
From choice of twelve you begged.
Your eye was keen, your tail well-curved,
You had your mother's legs –

So long – you had the speed of wind -
Outpaced the flock with ease.
I had to train you not to grab
The ewe, by leg or fleece!

But learn you did – and soon became
A colleague, not a pet.
We shared our thoughts, beliefs and fears,
Communication – yet

Eye contact got the message through:
'Times, brow to brow we rested
To share our understanding deep
Through days when we were tested.

Your fear of noise – your panic blind –
When gunshots loud retort.
The chewed front door was not your fault
You needed our support.

When we moved south and mistress died
You helped through stormy weather:

We walked the woods, you heard my sobs;
New heights we gained together.

And then we found a mistress new –
You listened for arrival;
With yelps of joy you met the car –
Companionship – revival.

But life moved on – the joints grew stiff -
The walking slow and laboured;
We still found ways to share our lives
Though rests between were favoured!

Then came the time, with breathing deep,
Your lungs began to struggle,
Sparse comfort then from lying down.
Your eyes transmit your trouble.

We had to part, sweet darling Star;
We humans walk alone now,
But midst the trees, your spirit lives,
Brings peace and memories – how

You shared your life, your joys, your smiles,
As only you could show;
Remembrances which stay with me
As still through life we go.

So farewell Star, my canine friend
I loved you from the start;
The life we shared, it brought us joy
Which lives on in my heart.

                                          Chris Sangster

CHAPTER EIGHT

STRUCTURING YOUR LIFE

Business Strategies for Life Adventures

SO FAR, we've considered various forms of balance or 'duality' in our lives – the *yin* and *yang*, positive and negative energies, darkness and light ... even loss and gain. As well as being conscious of the extremes of each pendulum swing, we should now be aware that it must always ultimately settle at an acceptable equilibrium point. This often takes longer than we expect – but it will finally happen. Dealing – 'coping' – with these extremes and finding the balance points should be one of our key goals in work and life. In the previous chapter I highlighted how many of the concepts encapsulated in business strategies and 'best practice' will help you foresee some of the potential pitfalls ahead – and avoid or at least limit your stressful falls into the pits!

Work–Life Balance

One of the key pairs of opposites that most of us have to deal with, to varying degrees, is what is usually referred to as work–life balance. I remember when it was originally proposed, it was seen in a very positive light – shorter working hours, more time to pursue leisure activities and a greater degree of flexibility as to when one worked. We would thus have more time to cope with our lives. In many ways, this has happened, but has been coloured by the missing part of that early equation – the availability of money.

Rather naively, the assumption was often that, though we would be working shorter hours, wages would remain the same or increase proportionally to allow us to fund our leisure activities. Around the same era, house ownership was craved as being the proverbial 'financial spaceship to the moon', with first-time buying and then subsequent trading up being the way forward financially for any who could afford it ... and many who could not.

It is this balance – and the holistic combination of work and life techniques and standards – which we will be focusing on for this chapter. Earlier, I proposed that the average person, in a life setting, would happily help others with advice, practical help or moral support. These qualities are also proposed in many team-building training exercises in business – but one hears regularly about the impersonal, inconsiderate and unacceptable management methods experienced in many companies. The surprise is that many of these assertive if inexperienced managers in business are likely to be the same positive, helpful people in the home environment. One must therefore assume that there are additional stresses and pressures at work which change Jekyll into Hyde!

'Work–life balance' is just what it says on the tin – an initiative to combine the best of both, for overall improvement. Many fluctuations are however involved!

Downshifting

In 2004, my late wife Gillean and I wrote a book extolling the virtues of 'downshifting', which I still firmly believe is a way forward for many. Downshifting is not opting out, and involves a change (usually a reduction or simplification) of overall lifestyle, rather than necessarily living a cheaper existence. Moving from Wiltshire to Scotland, for example, we actually 'upsized' in property terms – but it was so that we could use the property to run the holiday cottage business. In work terms, we both moved from being freelance consultants in our different skills (earning high day-rates!) to managing and servicing three cottages. In truth, I had previously downshifted when we moved from London to Wiltshire to become a writer and massage therapist, while Gil continued as a consultant, becoming the main breadwinner then.

We didn't earn a lot of money in Scotland. Our accountant (whom we knew from London days) could never quite understand how we made ends meet! We only had the three cottages – which is probably the bare minimum in commercial terms – although our location in the mountainous west coast meant we had climbers and walkers throughout the year. Overall, however, we had a much more flexible and enjoyable life than before, managing to share our lives and thoughts to a wonderful degree – and adjusting our needs and pursuits to match our budget. We also had more time to involve ourselves in community activities – Gillean in developing a local Heritage Centre, and me for five years chairing a committee that masterminded the building of a new Community Centre.

So, downshifting incorporates more focused expectations, coupled with lower outgoings, which provide a lifstyle where we can find a much greater opportunity really to get to know ourselves and establish a balance which is probably biased more towards life than work. It doesn't work for everyone, and there are many considerations and decisions to make. There are invariably bad times as well as good, but having a greater degree of direct control over your overall existence does help manage coping strategies. The chapters of our book (THE DOWNSHIFTER'S GUIDE TO RELOCATION) help the reader through these various reviews and decisions.

Love, Harmony and Service

After moving to Hampshire, I ran several weekend retreats with my colleague Jeremy Hayward (one of the principals at the White Eagle Lodge in Liss, which is near Petersfield) with the title 'Spirituality in the Workplace'. In this, we attempted to identify and combine the key priorities for coping with both work and life and how this involvement could achieve an overall benefit.

The key emphasis was in a study of how love, harmony and service in life could relate to personal interactions, team development and co-operation at work. The words and their normal understanding may be different but the sentiments are very similar.

Cross-fertilizing these different aspects and approaches certainly helped the participants on the retreats to establish, discuss and review strategies which could be applied to coping with the stresses of work and life – and responding to particular crises.

Perhaps we first need to consider what is meant by 'spirituality'. As far as applying it in life and work, definitions of spirituality vary, dependent on the source. Although a theologian might define it as 'the way we orientate ourselves towards the divine', many would maintain that it is possible to lead a spiritual way of life without following any particular religious path. Another proposal could be that 'spirituality can be seen as displaying and applying a heightening level of awareness towards others in a selfless and altruistic way'. In the book SPIRITUALITY IN THE WORKPLACE by Marques, Dhiman and King (published by Personhood Press), the authors propose the following definition:

> Spirituality in the workplace is an experience of interconnectedness among those involved in a work process, initiated by authenticity, reciprocity and personal goodwill; engendered by a deep sense of meaning that is inherent in the organization's work and resulting in greater motivation and organizational excellence.

Example – what Constitutes a 'Spiritual Person'?

These authors also quote the criteria which I proposed in an article published in the August 2003 edition of *Training Journal*. I argued that spiritual people are those who –

- Think co-operatively and/or altruistically
- Have a balanced, objective view of the world
- Listen as much as (or more than) they speak
- Apply three-dimensional, bigger-picture thinking
- Believe in some higher 'driving force' and purpose beyond humankind
- Think laterally in order to promote realistic solutions
- Encourage and empower others selflessly
- Work open-mindedly with a wide range of people

- *Consistently display integrity and trust*
- *Expect the best from people, without being taken advantage of.*

If you think about these criteria for a moment, many of them represent a fairly relaxed, contemplative way of life – displaying attitudes which are probably conducive to dealing objectively with crises and stress, as they affect yourself and impact on others. I believe that these criteria are equally valid for involvement in all aspects of life and work – whether applied inwardly by the individual or outwardly, in his or her dealings and relationships with others.

Spend a few moments considering the degree to which they encapsulate your current way of life – and those of your family and colleagues.

Before we move to specifics, I would like to quote from a White Eagle publication, PRAYER, MINDFULNESS AND INNER CHANGE. I would strongly recommend White Eagle's published teachings and have given contact details in the reference section. They are remarkably clear and easy to read and, although they were originally channelled by Grace Cooke some time ago, are equally relevant today.

The Spirit of Service

If you can, take this keynote out into your life tomorrow – the tomorrow which begins the life of the everyday, the life of workshop and factory, warehouses and offices and schools and the many varying phases of activity. Take into this world the will to serve. You do not work because you can get something by so doing; you work to serve. Many whom you contact, you will feel do not deserve your service and love. But remember, they may be suffering; they may have *sorrows of which you know not; their souls may be troubled. Bear then sympathy towards them. Many, as you travel the road of life, need your help.Your work, if you are to fulfil your creation, is to serve them with wisdom and love. It is this service which brings dignity and humility to the heart of man.*

White Eagle

In short, as well as responding to our own crises and trials, we should be aware of the problems and trials of others – and react sympathetically to them.

Love and Harmony

Love, harmony and service – in our workshop, we featured these aspects as being the keys to a more altruistic and un-selfish life.

We've already considered the applications of love in life to some great extent in chapter five. We considered the positive outcomes from the widespread volunteering and the open, non-egotistical attitudes of the athletes during the 2012 Olympics. We reviewed the implications of the shift from authoritative to co-operative methods in business; we considered the applications of altruism where it has moved from the personal ego to a much further-reaching view. We examined the applications of love and harmony in the Now moment, where assistance was offered as needed, without thoughts of return – as a positive energy and way of thinking towards others.

Speak openly about the concept of 'love' to many people in business and you'll receive strange looks. However, speak about respect, acknowledgement, pride, trust and understanding and they will at least accept the concepts – and probably manifest some of them at least, in their actions. Looking once more to the adage 'do as you would be done by', there isn't really any strong reason why activities and criteria which work in life should not be applicable in business – and *vice versa*. Applying this thinking will encourage the possibilities of prevention rather than cure, which we underlined earlier.

Example – the Foundations of Good Business Practices in Life

Some work environments do honour these standards – many in the creative areas of IT traditionally displayed relatively relaxed attitudes towards the working conditions, level and status of their staff. Charities and the voluntary sector also present the potential for dealing with staff and clients in special ways – although this perhaps requires greater endeavour in some quarters! As competition increases, however, purse strings and controls tighten, even in these work environments – but honest and co-operative work practices are more likely to continue, as long as the foundations are retained.

What are these business foundations?

- *Effective communication and listening*
- *Trust and freedom to encourage lateral thinking and decision-making*
- *A positive, supportive working environment*
- *Clear overall goals and established roles and responsibilities*
- *Awareness of the company's strategic plans (its 'bigger picture')*
- *A consistent management preparing the foundations for self-empowerment*

- *Open and honest two-way feedback, without 'hidden agendas'*
- *Unemotional debate leading towards potential compromise*

As an interesting exercise, consider the above business foundations as they would apply in family life as you know it. How could we 'translate' these business skills to help us cope more easily with the kinds of crises we're likely to encounter in daily family life?

For example, consider the management role as that of the parent(s), with the children taking on the employee role. Replace 'company's strategic plans' with the family's standards and expectations and most of the other statements can be directly transferred between business and family settings. People being the same, it's only right that the criteria shouldn't differ greatly … the more spiritually aware person will ensure that they don't.

Ponder on these applications for a moment, as a means of coping with life.

Giving Service Mindfully

With reference to the previous White Eagle quotation, let's return to the application of service. I've mentioned the quotation 'do as you would be done by' several times. In this service context, this doesn't mean doing work or service with the hope of gaining something directly in return – we do it to serve others. For a wide variety of reasons, many people need your help – just as, at other times, you will require help from others.

'Service' is all-encompassing. In business, senior management is as involved in servicing the company's needs as is the lowliest technician or cleaner. How? An effective manager is one who works hard to maintain the foundations, facilities and clear channels necessary to allow his/her staff to perform as efficiently and progressively as possible. A good manager makes things happen to clear the way for others to achieve – and to feel motivated by their achievements. When this background smoothing of the way happens, it works absolute wonders in reducing the presence of stressful situations.

Coping with any Service Deficiencies

Being realistic, however, there will still be times when the working environment is not as positive as might be desired. Where work and life relationships are less than ideal, stressful 'nettles' will encroach on your path. These stresses will have a direct effect upon you, where, for example, demands are made which you would ideally not find to be acceptable. The world, sadly, is not always ideal!

'Me Time' at Work

I've come across lots of people who work through their lunch breaks, work much longer hours than they're contracted (and paid) to do and remain in contact with their place of work even when on holiday. I've even come across people who don't take their full holiday entitlement each year! The usual reason given is that the supervisor/team leader/manager/company or whatever expects it and that things would act against the person if he or she refused. This is wrong.

Generally, companies stick religiously to Health and Safety standards in physical and operational terms. In truth, this may often be largely because they can be fined if they don't. I would suggest that these stressful working conditions, created by placing requirements above and beyond contracted job agreements are equally a Health issue and, arguably, could be monitored in the same way as, for example, tachographs record lorry drivers' hours.

Consider scheduling in some 'me time' to your day. Build in any controls you can, to make your working day more manageable and less stressful. Use any breaks – especially your lunch break – to move away from your work station. A change of atmosphere promotes a change of attitude, with both likely to be positive. The old Japanese 'salaryman' style where no one leaves the office until the boss leaves is, frankly, ridiculous. Don't get involved in or accept anything similar!

Coping by Saying 'No' ... Politely!

This may be hard to do – and there are subtle ways of doing it, of course – but there's only a finite amount you can achieve in any given day. Being known as the person who will always accept extra work means that it is likely to continue to pile up on you. This might stimulate your ego initially but can become very stressful in the long term. In real terms, there are only so many nettles you can grasp. Learn to say 'No'!

Prioritizing is something we will consider more deeply later – at this juncture, all we need to know is that it can be used in such situations to establish a finite quantity and sequence of work that you can fairly be expected to achieve during the day. If something new turns up, an existing piece of work will therefore have to be pushed further down the overall pile, to be completed the next day. If you work for one boss, this is reasonably easy to negotiate, saying something along the lines of – 'I can complete "A" or "B' today. Which is more important to you?' Where your workload involves different originators, negotiation becomes more complicated.

The most important thing initially, is getting your head round the fact that you can take some control. You can say 'No' – you're not being selfish but are ensuring that you can maintain your personal standards, within the bigger picture. You're part of a wider team of people, in life as well as work. There will usually be someone else who can take on the task if you are genuinely fully occupied with alternative, equally (or more) important tasks. There may be someone who is better skilled to do it. You must of course remain flexible – there will be unique crises which do require extra effort – but when crises are appearing almost daily, invariably at the last moment, it's time to take a stance!

Sealing

There is another technique which is used in a slightly more spiritual context – it's also appropriate where involved with a therapy incorporating energies. In my early days as a masseur, when I hadn't perfected it, I picked up some very negative and stressful 'vibes' from some patients, causing severe headaches.

Sealing is the act of visualizing yourself encased in a ball of white light, which acts as a protection against external influences. It's something to do initially, to develop your inner strength and build protection, rather than wrapping yourself later, as (in a way) bandaging a wound! Once again – prevention rather than cure.

There's a good exercise for practising this grounding near the start of Colum Hayward's book THE MEDITATION LIFE-STYLE – taking the time to initially ground and seal yourself in this way is very valuable towards gaining future protection. It may cause surprise to see that recommended in the workplace, but it may be precisely where it's most wanted. Sealing takes a bit of imagination and effort to do, with success probably coming progressively but it's worth the effort. Once you've established a belief in or acceptance of the principles, you may find that you will almost automatically imagine a protective wall, ball, bubble or whatever image works for you, when confronted by a stressful situation involving others.

This sealing was also an initial element of the 'Slide Fader' coping strategy which we reviewed in chapter three. Bringing yourself to the 'Now' state, where you consciously retreat into your body, evacuating the mind, is an extreme example of imagining yourself to be surrounded by this white light protection. If it helps you to cope with potentially stressful situations – consider it as part of your 'toolbox' of strategies. If it seems a little 'off the wall' at the moment, hold it in reserve for some future time – when you might find yourself in the position where you consider it possible and useful.

Managing your Goals in Life

One business strategy which has direct applications in life generally is goal-setting. In running the 'Spirituality in the Workplace' workshop, however, I would say this was the subject area where we experienced most problems. Some delegates found it very difficult to be specific enough about their personal goals, while others reacted negatively because it made them acutely conscious of some past goals which they hadn't completed successfully. One or two saw goal setting as nettles which were just too painful to embrace initially. We had one or two cases where it required the passage of several months after the workshop, before the benefits of a degree of strategic planning through goal-setting gradually won through.

So, you may take some time completing your personal goals properly – in fact you may revisit the exercise a few times over the next months. That's fine – but do persevere, because the strategic planning involved gives long-lasting outcomes ... ultimately!

Planning a Sequence of Now Goals

Think of the sequence as being like a packet of sliced bread, with each slice a Now experience. The far end of the packet will thus represent the end goal. Evidently, we do need to be clear what this end goal is before starting off through the individual Now slices. Each slice will represent an action which has to be completed, with a logical progression through the slices.

Unsurprisingly, as we saw in our earlier visualization of the path with milestones in chapter five, progress is more complex than eating our way progressively through a sliced loaf from beginning to end!

So, how does it work, in reality? Let's consider an example.

Example: Steps and Stages towards a Goal

Many people have the dream of 'being their own boss', as a means of being able to cope better with working life. They feel that this will allow them to make decisions which they can support and act upon – in short, that they're more in control of their personal destiny. Although this might be the single, final objective that they're heading towards, it will incorporate a sequence of goals which build towards that final point.

So, for the purpose of this exercise, let's consider how you would go about achieving the goal of becoming self-employed within five years.

Bear in mind that, when you're 'drilling down' into the steps and stages of this, you must keep an awareness of not only the end point but also the timings involved; how you'll be able to monitor your progress; the kinds of priorities which you must incorporate and the different techniques you can apply to keep things moving forward.

So, what might be the sequence of actions along the way, towards achieving your goal of becoming successfully self-employed? (This is only one interpretation, which is offered as a guideline. You may have different priorities. Don't accept it blindly – use it as a framework to establish your own understandings of priorities and sequence.)

One possible sequence (or business plan) might be:

- Identify your personal strengths and skills
- Establish which is/are the most marketable
- Select or identify a specific business opportunity
- Evaluate the strength of your market (locally and regionally)
- Consider whether to buy an existing business or start from scratch

- Estimate the purchase or start-up costs for setting up your business
- Discuss the availability of finance, reviewing any options
- Decide on best location(s) for your chosen business
- Research properties/facilities required
- Visit area(s) and review competition, relative to properties, etc.
- Identify and contact local suppliers
- Agree on premises/facilities, with contractual agreements
- Arrange for any design and fitting out of premises
- Establish operating strategies, any staff requirements, etc.
- If there are additional staff, arrange recruitment, HR organization, etc.
- Decide launch date and arrange advertising/marketing
- Set up facility ready for trading activity.

This plan-sequence is not cast in stone. Some actions will logically follow on from previous ones, while some could run in parallel or substitute, to reduce the effects of any blockages, time delays and so on. Some may not be relevant to particular areas of self-employment – in other words, use it as guidelines but really think through your own personal applications.

Establishing your personal goals (towards self-employment in this example – but it can be applied for all types of different situations) takes time and quite complex planning and decision-making. It's well worth the effort, because, having drafted out your possible sequences of events, you have an ever-available checklist of where you are in the process; what needs to be done and when – and the range of other operational checks you need to keep on top of. With a little help from one of the various business advisers available (Google the words 'business advice' for support local to you) your ideas will be only a few simple steps away from being crafted into a business plan – necessary if you wish to apply for any grants, bank loans or other forms of support out there waiting for you.

The Basic Steps and Stages of Progress

I'd like to end this chapter with one final structure, which can be widely applied in both work and life environments. It gives a reference structure which you can use to build strategies, giving you added confidence to cope with those periodic nettles.

Like much wisdom, it's quite simple and straightforward when you think about it – the secret is to think about it! In Buddhist teaching, there is a sequence covering the names *pariyatta, patipatta* and *pativeda* – assimilation, practice and realization. This and the business sequence below are methods of checking where you are along your development path or sequence of goals. They also allow you to establish a clearer idea of what the next steps are. As the application of following sequence helps you review your progress more confidently, it can be seen as yet another coping strategy for your 'toolbox' of techniques.

Firstly, the steps are –

BELONGING > ASSERTION > CO-OPERATION

This is what each stage means -

Belonging involves being at a stage where you are comfortable with a situation and feel confident and assured.

Assertion comes where your confidence encourages you to want more – to put yourself forward for additional activities, to prove to yourself and others that you are competent.

Co-operation is established where your confidence allows you to work happily with others, with mutual respect shown and experience reinforcing skills and awareness.

In any situation, it's likely that you may be involved in doing different things at the same time. You could, for example, be working co-operatively in certain skills areas while, at the same time, asserting yourself to gain experience in other skills.

Notice also that assertion as described here is positive but not aggressive. Unfortunately, many of us will potentially recall someone whose assertiveness is rather 'pushy' and aggressive. As I'm describing it, it is a natural, positive progression where the individual is seeking wider experience to maintain his or her motivation, without pushing people aside in the process. It's a means of allowing the individual to feel more in control – to be able to cope more confidently with crises that come his/her way. It gives a progression and structure for grasping those nettles more confidently!

Notice also that the latter levels – of realization and co-operation – involve the greatest degree of unselfish and altruistic thought. It's a longer and harder interval to this next milestone on your wisdom path progression – but well worth the continuing struggle!

Let's consider some applications.

Examples of the Belonging/Assertion/
Co-operation Continuum

1. Job Progress

Initially, a new starter needs to have his or her basic and safety needs satisfied, in order to feel that he or she belongs in the organization. As well as having a desk or work location, he or she should have some meaningful work (but not too taxing, initially) so as to feel a useful member of the team. He or she should also be provided with a reference point to establish working practices and facilities which may be provided by a 'buddy' or mentor.

As time advances, the employee should gain confidence and, if motivated, will begin to assert him- or herself by seeking more responsibility, asking to go on development courses and even taking the initiative to complete additional tasks. If this is supported by management, this assertion by the employee is a positive development, where he or she is beginning to reveal true competencies, skills and aspirations. Patience is required, because these developmental opportunities don't happen overnight, but employee persistence should win through, where management encouragement is present.

Having reached a point where new skills need to be implemented, the employee is likely to want to work co-operatively with others, to reinforce these skills. There will still be an element of ongoing self-improvement, which will manifest as occasional flurries of assertion, in order to maintain progress.

2. Team Development

When building a team, where there are different responsibilities to be met, it's important that each team member feels that he or she belongs, by having a clearly defined role. Where each role impacts on others, time must be spent discussing how integration will work, so that the individual roles will fit together comfortably, without too much overlap.

The team leader should be ready to 'feed' the assertive

desires of team members, as they occur by ensuring that additional tasks and integrated activities are available, which once again fit into the team framework without clashing too much. It's at this stage, where individuals can become too pro-active or frustrated at the slower pace of others, that assertion can degenerate slightly to incorporate some degree of aggression.

If team members' development has been handled effectively in these earlier stages, with team reviews and one-to-ones carried out to reinforce acceptable practice, the team should reach the stage of being capable of working co-operatively. At this point, individual inputs should feed into the overall activities and outcomes of the team. If the team leader has done the groundwork – and continues to reinforce standards and acceptable practices where there are any individual lapses – the team should become very effective, leaving the team leader largely free to prepare the conditions for continued effectiveness, at management and other organizational meetings.

3. Family Development

As the child grows through its initial years, an atmosphere of safety and belonging is very important. The child should have as much contact with the parents – with the maternal role probably being more important in the initial years – and experience established routines. A peaceful, positive environment also helps to reinforce belonging.

As the years pass, the child is likely to become more assertive, potentially becoming aggressive at times where parental controls are being implemented. The trick here is for the parents to manage the assertion positively, providing the facilities and support for the child to assert him- or herself creatively or through sport, for example, as well as allowing some degree of (monitored) freedom to develop.

On maturation from child to young adult, the individual is likely to become more co-operative within the family unit. If developed as an active family member at the earlier stages, the co-operative young adult can become a delight, entering into family discussions and involving him- or herself in day-to-day family activities.

Thus, any situation where people are interacting will benefit from an awareness of this model, to allow inter-relationships to be monitored and individual needs supported. If this supervision is maintained, many of the stresses which otherwise might be calling for remedial coping strategies, will rarely or never see the light of day.

Like the bell curve we considered earlier, the belonging/assertive/co-operative model is applicable in most situations – giving a structure which helps us understand what is (or should be) happening and can therefore be used to prevent or alleviate many crises. It is well worth using as a strategic framework for our planning and responses.

Meditative Thought: through 'Business Poetry'

For this chapter, I've selected the poem overleaf, which was published in the 'Echoes' Work section of my two-part inspirational, work–life balance book-set MESSAGES FROM THE MOUNTAINS and ECHOES IN THE ATRIUM.

It underlines the importance of getting work–life balance right.

Working that Life-Balance Thing

Working long or working smart,
Stretching brain or straining heart,
Chasing targets, as they move,
Merely so that we can prove
That we're team players, know the range,
We can cope with constant change,
Work the extra hours they ask
And welcome those additional tasks
Because it shows we play the game –
Support the boss, accept the blame,
When we don't follow shifting posts
Or fail to second-guess, at most.

While meantime, back in family nest,
Our partners do their level best
To compensate for lack of dad
Or mum – which makes the children sad.

Work–life balance – that's the way:
We need to sort out how we play
As well as work, protect our health –
Equal surely to the wealth
We strive to increase, house to pay –
Looking forward to the day
When we retire – then we can live,
With work behind us, we can give
No further thought to business tasks.

But now the question we should ask –
'How many people can we name
Whose latter years, they sadly came
And went with an untimely pace?'
Through illness, even death to face,
Their work–life balance didn't blend:
They'd burned their candle at both ends.

This balance thing is not just time
You spend in office, site or line,
It's how you function, day-to-day
It's how you think, it's what you say,
It's looking past the basic acts
Which grind upon us: make the pact
To see the picture, bigger, planned –
Apply your logic, take in hand
Priorities which you believe
Will help you confidently leave
Behind the crap which you once stood –

Achieve the balance, for common good!

Chris Sangster

CHAPTER NINE

ADDRESSING THE NETTLES OF PAIN, STRESS AND FEAR

Stressing the Positive

What is stress? How can we cope?
Not the time to give up hope
We plan, refine, prioritize
Matching actions to the size
And grandeur of each new demand
However scheduled – seldom planned.

Why train to counter this confusion?
Chaos caused oft through collusion
'Tween bosses who, at their command
Assume that we have time in hand,
Will loosely meet their needs ahead
By pulling rank, scrape through instead.

If, in lieu of this sorry state,
They learned to plan and co-operate,
Discuss our needs, respect the skills
Of those relied on to fulfil
The output which the team all know
Will meet the deadlines; let us grow

> In pride and stature, skills as well
> Then, once the stressful levels fell,
> We all could balance work and life,
> Spend more time with the husband, wife
> Or partner, kids – have hobbies too
> To be more 'rounded' people who
>
> Refreshed, relaxed, could start the days
> At work – with planned priorities,
> Which give a structure to the tasks
> We must complete – too much to ask?
>
> I do not think so, if we all can
> But think of others – and forward plan.
>
> *Chris Sangster*

It seemed appropriate to start the chapter with this poem – one of the first 'business poems' I wrote – because it links together so many of the subjects we have been considering so far.

We all speak about our involvement with pain, stress and fear from time to time – but their effects come in different degrees and elicit different responses. I've already suggested that some element of stress (in the form of a degree of nervousness) can sometimes be a 'good thing' – for example when giving a presentation – as it can make you try that little bit harder!

In a similar way, a degree of pain in your ankle, for example, is your body reminding you that all is not well down there and that you should be taking care not to stress it physically until the pain subsides. There was a sports-mad lady who used to come regularly to our Scottish cottages for hill walking. Invariably, she would have some injury from a previous skiing or kayaking holiday, with her response being to dose up with pain killers so that she could 'hit the mountains running'. I tried to underline the error of her ways for the longer term.

Even an element of fear, when we're out walking along a dark street or forest path, will keep us on edge, ready with our fight or flight reaction if anything untoward should happen. There's an interesting quotation on the subject from the Tibetan, Djwhal Khul (channelled by Alice A Bailey) from PON-DER ON THIS – a magical reference book of erudite quotations which every thinking adult should have by their bedside.

Fear

Fear is the product of ignorance and in its initial stages it is not the product of wrong thinking. It is basically instinctual and is found dominating in the non-mental animal kingdom, as well as in the human kingdom. But in the human, its power is increased potentially through the powers of the mind, and through memory of past pain and grievance, and anticipation of those we foresee, the power of fear is enormously aggravated by the thought-form we ourselves have built of our own individual fears and phobias. This thought-form grows in power as we pay attention to it, for 'energy follows thought', till we become dominated by it.

Djwhal Khul (The Tibetan)

As we're beginning to bring things together in this chapter, you may recall our considerations of different responses to pain. Controlling pain in the Now moment, we were recommending that any thought of future related problems was not helpful. Remember also the slide-fader coping strategy aimed at drawing our focus within that protective bubble, while slowing down our metabolism.

Embracing Nettles

Recall our image of the track, alongside which beds of nettles appear periodically. Often, we'll consciously keep away from them; at other times we may brush carefully against them, while ensuring that we're protected from direct contact. Yet again, we may sometimes cautiously push them aside with our bare hands, knowing that any immediate discomfort will soon be forgotten. Sometimes we'll embrace them carefully – and sometimes, we'll grasp hold of them and break the stems, getting them out of our path, once and for all.

Example: Different Levels of Response

And moreover, how do we decide which strategy is appropriate for these various levels of opposition? The decision will rest on the answers to a range of questions.

- *To what extent is it impeding my progress?*
- *What would happen if I didn't carry out this particular activity?*
- *Is there an alternative way to achieve my goal?*
- *If I've no choice but to accept, are there any provisos I would wish to emphasize?*
- *What would be the effects on me if I stood up to this – short and long-term?*

- *Who are the people who are immediately affected by this situation?*
- *What are the implications to them (and me) if I refuse to do something?*
- *What alternative solutions might I propose, which would suit my needs better?*
- How do I decide what to do, if the suggested activity is 'against my principles'?
- How do I say 'No', without creating offence (or do I risk offending)?

In terms of refusing to do things, I'm not fomenting revolution here! As we saw earlier in 'Saying 'No'', you can refuse in a pleasant and constructive way, in terms of not being comfortable doing option 'A' – but willing to compromise on option 'B'. You could establish that, physically, you can't fit this extra task into the day's work, so something will have to be delegated to someone else – or done tomorrow. You could underline that the requested action is more the responsibility of someone else, who should therefore be tasked to do it (and their refusal is no reason why you should do it!)

If you're clear about what you should be doing, and what you are proficient at doing, you can be confident about what you can do best and what will be better done by someone else, for these various reasons.

Pain, Stress and Fear

Let's consider each of these in turn, beginning with **Pain**.

Some people endure almost constant pain to varying degrees. You might feel that you're suffering badly with a nagging toothache, which perhaps needs a periodic aspirin or ibuprofen to keep the pain at bay – but then you might meet someone who has shingles, psoriasis, an amputation or one of any number of more serious conditions with which they have to cope. You then should begin to realize that everything is relative.

It would appear that people have differing pain thresholds – the level at which they can endure pain relatively comfortably (if that doesn't sound like a contradiction in terms!) Somewhat to my surprise, during my spell in hospital I discovered that I have a fairly high pain threshold – but I also have a vivid imagination (I write poetry, after all, so I guess that's to be expected!) And so was born my fader technique as a coping strategy.

Example: the Pain of Needles

As I've already confessed, I have always had a problem with needles and injections. The doctors and nurses always said, 'you'll feel a sharp prick' – and indeed, that was all it was. There really was virtually no pain at all, so I analysed that the problem was therefore my imagination ... perhaps coupled with some bad experience in the subconscious past. So, my coping strategy of shutting down from thinking in the past and focusing on the Now moment – but not looking at the needle – worked admirably.

I lost count of the number of injections and blood samples I had – although things became easier, first with the insertion of a cannula (a needle permanently in the vein, with a one-way 'valve', allowing needles to be easily inserted) and subsequently a PICC line (which was similar but with a tube inserted directly into a vein and pushed closer to the heart.) The first line didn't work because the tube kinked in some way, so they had to put a second one in.... I'm amazed in retrospect how all these interventions went so smoothly! I got into the way of silently asking for help from my spirit guides (which in time became, rather irreverently: 'OK boys, I need your help here!') but it certainly seemed to do the trick! Strangely enough, I'm still unable to watch images on TV of someone being injected, so the psychological, imaginative situation evidently still exists.

Although I was in a permanent septic state for the first ten days while they tried a variety of antibiotics to tackle the bacteria (which included one very obscure one which I might have picked up from an old wooden South American flute I'd bought on eBay), the only real pain I was experiencing was when I tried to swallow. I was well looked after.

Pain Management

Nowadays, where people are experiencing fairly constant pain, they tend to enter a programme of pain management. This helps greatly with coping. In hospital, pain killers such as paracetamol are freely offered where any pain is experienced and I was connected to a morphine pump while in Intensive Care (although I didn't actually use it much at all). So, although degrees of pain will vary, there are medical ways of coping, as well as some of the previously-suggested internal relief strategies in chapter three. At the other extreme from 'sharp pricks' and discomfort, the constant, nagging or longer-duration pains are harder to cope with. Perhaps it's not a particularly serious pain you're experiencing – it's the incessant nature of it which gets to you and can wear you down, so any strategy (including medication) which can override this constant assault will be welcome.

Distraction

Another pain-control strategy, which has long been known to work especially well with children, is distraction. Most mothers will tell you, when their infant is crying, that showing them a toy, making different sounds or even just shifting the baby's position, will stop the crying (unless, of course, the pain is genuinely more extreme). Distraction works with adults as well – when ill, if you're sitting or lying around doing nothing but thinking about your illness and pain, it can become all-consuming. Distraction through music, conversation, TV, reading or some mild activity if appropriate can often help the patient forget the pain to some extent at least.

This is yet another example of focusing on the 'Now' moment and shutting down on any thinking about what might happen in the future. Personally, I try to use chemical pain relief as little as possible, to give the greatest effect when I really need it – but that's my choice. Develop a coping strategy which works for you, relative to your situation.

Stress

There are many causes and degrees of stress and, as with pain, some people can cope healthily with more stress than others. There are schools of thought which propose that some stress is 'good for you' – I was suggesting earlier that a minor feeling of stress and fear can 'up your game' where appropriate. But stress can of course reach much more serious proportions, causing an inability to function effectively and potentially a degeneration into ill health.

What is one of the key causes of stress? It's often the feeling of powerlessness – where there are factors which are outside your control and which are causing problems to which you might find it hard to respond. So, we can consider general coping strategies but these might have only limited effectiveness in specific situations. It's often down to combining ideas from your 'toolbox' to respond to the particular problem, once analysed.

Example: a New IT Consultancy Project

I worked as a subcontractor on a consultancy project, for a call-centre type of company which was upgrading its complete IT (information technology) system. Our training input was to develop staff training programmes to implement the system but, as deadlines approached, the actual system design wasn't complete because the client company kept wanting new add-ons – which is a common problem that several national projects have also experienced.

The project manager from the training consultancy company wasn't on site and visited each Friday, for meetings with the client, after which she invariably called us together to tell us that much of our completed work was no longer applicable, as the plans had changed. As the deadline grew ever closer, the company's training manager (who was the direct liaison link) mysteriously disappeared and I was seconded in his place (I subsequently discovered that he was in hospital, having had a nervous breakdown!).

The senior director wouldn't postpone the 'go live' date, or review the decision to shut down the old system on that date, rather than implement the transition gradually; the system was being designed by a company in Israel, while documentation was being produced by a company in New Zealand; I found myself shuttling between meetings to the extent that I didn't have time between them to pursue actions.… I could go on, but I imagine you've got the picture that it was a chaotic, stressful situation. Over time, I began to dread going to work each morning and, when I found myself sitting rocking on the bathroom floor one morning, I decided that enough was enough. I handed in my notice and resigned, as I considered my sanity to be more important than any contract.

Resignation

Applying this is at the extreme end of coping with stress – but is always an option. In some ways, it's easier to carry out as a consultant or contractor but I've implemented it as a direct employee in a company as well, where I could not accept the company's dubious standards and criteria. It takes nerve to do, as it evidently can cause parallel stress in maintaining your financial position (and potentially creating a 'black mark' on your future CV, in the eyes of others). If it seems an option, approach it carefully – you may be able to negotiate some settlement or line up another job first – or at least give yourself time to accumulate some money to tide you over after resignation, until you find another job. I've always considered that working conditions with low levels of stress are very important – largely because it allows me to feel in control of my actions and priorities to some large extent.

Distorted Expectations

To some people, there is almost a special kudos in having a 'high-stress job' or in continually working long, stressful hours beyond the legal requirement. It makes such people feel indispensable to their employer, until such time as they perhaps discover they're 'being let go' because there are other, younger colleagues, who may cope with the stressful demands – and perform – better. And so, the constant watching over the shoulder becomes stressful in its own right.

As with my example above, a lot of stress in business is caused by management styles which pay little attention to the real health and wellbeing of staff members. Many companies will have policies in place to respond to severe stress in an employee when it finally surfaces – but little emphasis on monitoring the deficiencies in individual management techniques which are causing it. As we considered in a previous exercise, some people will seek out self-employment as a means of 'being one's own boss', reducing the stress caused by unacceptable management decisions from above – but unfortunately, they may then experience new stress through financial problems or lack of work.

'TYPE A' Stress

A study of different types of managers was carried out by the researchers Friedman and Rosenman. They came up with a profile of what they referred to as the 'Type A' manager (or more generally in life, person) as one who 'is hard-driving and demanding, both of self and others. He or she is ambitious, particularly in the material sense and highly competitive. He or she works under pressure and always appears rushed. He or she is strongly absorbed in the 24/7 culture and is more likely to be critical, hostile and undemonstrative.'

I can think of some managers who would be proud to think they fit this 'Type A' profile (apart perhaps from being critical and hostile!). In the study, these criteria are being regarded as stress-inducing – and are therefore not characteristics which we should strive to copy. Where already present, they need to be at the least, controlled.

The characteristics include rushing into an activity without due planning or 'bigger picture' thinking; being bad at controlling the amount of work they agree to accept (for themselves but invariably also for those who report to them directly); being poor at delegation and at assessing the quality of the work they achieve (focusing more on the quantity) and displaying low concern for interpersonal skills and communication.

From what we have already discussed, we can spot that these work practices will be likely to cause high levels of stress, both for the managers concerned and for their directly reporting staff and work colleagues.

Some indicators that you are a 'Type A' person:

- You tend to feel rushed
- You focus on key tasks and don't have wide interests
- You talk faster than normal and talk more than you listen when in a group
- You want to walk faster than others in the group
- You tend to finish other people's sentences or interrupt them when speaking
- You need to have the TV or radio on permanently
- You spend your time 'networking' for contacts at parties
- You tend to multi-task
- You are critical of the actions of others
- You are impatient with others when describing how to do tasks.

If some (or all!) of this rings true, it's time to step back and review your priorities somewhat. However much you think you're 'hitting the ground running' in an impressive way, be assured you're building up stress and future problems. Think of your priorities.

The research from Friedman and Rosenman does of course include reference to 'Type B' management styles, as well as additional information, should you be interested in investigating these aspects further (see book list in the Resources Section). In this chapter, we're focusing on stress – so I've featured the 'type A' profile featured by the researchers, as this gives us the strongest ammunition!

Prioritization

Let's start with what most of us will already know. I imagine we've all been involved with 'things to do' lists. My desk has got several lying around at any given moment; my fridge door has a list of DIY activities which are needed around the house (which doesn't reduce to any impressive extent, unfortunately!) and my diary is speckled with future actions which I have scheduled over the following months. Many involve quite brief, easily-achieved activities, while others are longer-term.

'Things to do' lists work – to a certain degree anyway. Where do they have problems? The problem is likely to be you, frankly! And me – all of us. Why? Because we may tend towards picking out the tasks that we like to do ahead of the tasks we need to do. This is where prioritization steps up to the line. Picture having two columns at the side of your 'things to do' list, one headed *Need to Do*, while the other is *Nice to Do*. If you can lay hands on one of your own lists at this moment, try separating your tasks using these two criteria.

'Need to do' in a home context involves things like completing your tax return, sending in the details of that supermarket order which is due to be delivered tomorrow, contacting a plumber to mend your toilet cistern or arranging a meeting to discuss a border dispute with your neighbour. These are all important things that need to be sorted out now – or in the near future. Leaving them 'pending' can become stressful – they can rapidly become nettles!

'Nice to do' activities are second division – like painting the hall, arranging for a trip to the cinema, buying some new plants for the front garden border or checking through brochures to plan next summer's holiday. They're all things that need to be done ultimately but they can be pushed down the list by higher (need to do) priorities. This leads us to the concept of having a sliding priority scale.

When might a 'Nice to' or 'B' become a 'Need to' or 'A' priority? When, for example, the trip to the cinema is in celebration of the eight-year-old's birthday, perhaps involving a party of ten. Forget that and see where you find yourself! Some systems use As, Bs and Cs to subdivide levels. We don't need to get bogged down in categorizing too finely – the important thing is to spend the time considering the relative timings and keep reviewing regularly. It's likely that a 'B' or 'C' task can sit there for several days as low priority but will need to be escalated to an 'A' task as the deadline approaches.

Prioritization can also be used within any particular category (of 'A' tasks, for example). Some of these tasks will be more important than others, for a variety of possible reasons. The key one is often that there is a deadline attached but there could be other reasons, such as the importance of the outcome to the company or household.

Keep an active watch on your various priority lists – they're a great way of maintaining a better control on your life. It is, of course, important to maintain and overall balance – life is not all 'A' priority tasks! This is where work–life balance considerations should come to the fore – reducing stress by achieving your high-priority tasks in time, while maintaining your sanity and joy of life by incorporating lower level (but relaxing and enjoyable) activities.

Checking for the Signs

We should be looking out for signs of 'slippage' in our achievement of priority tasks, to control any build-up of stress. With the best will in the world, however, these slippages will occur because of personal or external problems: identifying them as soon as possible will help you towards a timely response … and a reduction in stress levels.

What I'm underlining here is that we can take a leaf out of the 'business best-practice' book and look towards prevention rather than cure. Be conscious of the signs. Look out for them – and respond as best you can, as soon as you can.

Coping, as we're applying in the title of this book, incorporates channelling and slowing the tide of problems as they flow into the estuary, as best as we can, rather than waiting for the waves to erode and flood the banks further upriver.

Hold that image in your mind!

Talking Helps

Financial matters, caring for an elderly parent or sick member of the family, teenage and family problems, work-related issues affecting your ability to cope with home life, legal and/or attendance at court and home structural/ maintenance issues: all these are situations where we can hit the stressful dead ends. Behind most of them, though, there exist advisory services which you can access to talk through your problem and establish possible solutions.

As we've said, one of the key issues is the extent to which you feel in control of the situation. On many occasions, any isolation which may be felt can be alleviated if you seek out these agencies, support groups or even a close friend to talk to about the problem. These conversations are unlikely to come up with instant solutions but they do certainly help to get the matter out in the open. Sometimes it's only by talking through situations with someone, that the extent and/or real issues of the problem are revealed.

Stress – Keeping on Top of Situations

Sticking up for your principles; taking financial care not to live beyond your means; living as healthy a life as you can, with good diet and exercise regimes; spending time with your family to ensure that they're not 'going off the rails' in any way; maintaining your property regularly to prevent major problems with the structure and services: these are all methods of continuously keeping on top of stressful situations, which should reduce the need to become involved in major stress coping strategies. As they say, 'prevention is better than cure'!

Fear

Much fear comes from previous experiences we've had or heard about – or through our imagination of how things might evolve in the future. Through these areas of consciousness, we build images – which we construct from those individual fears and phobias. We've referred to several examples in the course of this book, from fear of how an illness might develop, to fear of physical attack.

Example – Fear of the Unknown

After my hospital experience, many people said to me, 'you must have been terribly afraid in there', or offered permutations of that remark. Strangely, I never felt any fear throughout the whole experience, which I consider was largely down to focusing consistently on each 'Now' situation or procedure. Taking the situation in a positive light, I was rather looking forward to experiencing an out-of-body experience at some point or encountering a dazzling bright light – but neither occurred. My visualized journeys down the white light corridor always ended with me coming up against an ornately-finished door, which remained firmly closed! When I considered this rationally later, I realized it was probably a good thing that I wasn't allowed to travel too far down that light corridor – I may not have been around to write this book, among other things!

I considered that I was totally aware of what was going on (apart from when I was under general anaesthetic, of course) but, on reflection, was undoubtedly in a mentally altered state from time to time in the early ten septic days, when my body experienced some fairly dramatic 'spikes' in vital signs, causing concern among the medical staff.

The only potentially fearful moment came during my time in Intensive Care when, as a result of the doctors' daily visit, my dedicated nurse was actioned to remove the drainage tube from the cavity surrounding my heart. I could see from her eyes that this was a new and stressful experience for her but that she didn't want to lose face by asking for help. As it was a case of potentially losing my heart or her face, I took the initiative of asking one of the doctors to help her! I was pleased I did because, observing them working together at close quarters – it was in my chest, after all! –

they appeared to need at least three hands to manipulate the parallel draining and removal procedures. The potential fear was eliminated by remaining in control and establishing a strategy to satisfy that 'Now' moment!

From subsequent conversation with various medical people, I now recognize that I was in much more of a life-threatening situation than I realized. In a post-operative interview, I was given the statistic that, apparently, an intensive care patient has around a fifty:fifty chance of returning to a normal ward and achieving longterm survival. This, and similar pearls of wisdom I have subsequently seen, makes me even more convinced about the additional benefits of the healing energies I received from all my light workers!

Would I have been more fearful if I'd been aware of this at the time of being a patient? Dealing positively with each day as it came, I reckon I would have been convinced I was to be one of the live fifty percent! I think my meditative, contemplative state helped me greatly – coupled with an open trust in the quality treatment I was receiving from the Queen Alexandra Hospital in Portsmouth.

Fear in Known and Unknown Situations

We can easily think of a wide variety of fearful situations – not having enough money to pay outstanding bills; approaching a situation where you have to discuss something disagreeable with a potential adversary; having a near miss while driving; walking towards a group of rowdy individuals who might turn aggressive; fear of the unknown, including death; dealing with gas, water or electrical problems at home, where things could go dramatically wrong … the list is wide and varied and could go on and on.

White Eagle again

I have a rather a nice quotation from a new White Eagle Publishing Trust book entitled CHAKRAS, AURAS, SUBTLE BODIES, which says:

> One of the important tests is that of fearlessness – how many of you have had the experience of coming up against something very undesirable in your sleep? Perhaps an animal may threaten to destroy you, with the result that you have had the feeling of running away as fast as you could go – and sometimes legs won't go! Oh, the panic and the fearsome things which threaten you! If only the individual would turn round and face the pursuer, nothing could harm him or her; the pursuer would vanish. So long as you run, of course, it will follow.
>
> Translate this to life. Grasp your nettle boldly. People want to run from things they dislike, instead of facing up to them. Face them and the terror goes and you are able to say 'How foolish I was to be frightened – why, it is nothing'.

Fearful Situations

As I hope I've established by now, we can do a lot to help and prepare ourselves for how we can choose to react to these fearful situations, when we turn to face them. We may already have had some experience of them – so, even if it's learning from our previous mistakes, it's possible that we can better prepare ourselves to meet the new 'Now' situation. We may have been able to prepare some possible strategies, so any latent fear can be diminishing rather than growing as we progress through the stages of dealing with the current 'Now' moment.

Unknown situations are different, in some ways anyway. Turning our justification on its head, because we don't have any past experience to compare and contrast – or even potentially learn lessons from – we've no 'blueprint' to follow. Think of explorers in the old days, setting off across an open sea, with no idea where they were going – or if there was even land over the horizon. Focusing on the 'Now' will help us cope with these types of situation, encouraging us to review active strategies towards coping currently, rather than dwell on past or future problems.

Fear of Dying

It's generally held that one of the greatest fears of all is the fear of dying. To many, this is the ultimate 'unknown'. There are many books written on the subject and I wouldn't want to undervalue the feelings people have through dealing with it briefly and simplistically. I remember my father, when lying composed and near death, suddenly opening his eyes and saying 'Oh, it's wonderful!', having presumably seen the way forward. I take that as an encouragement!

Of course, in many, many cases, it's the period of potentially painful deterioration between the last normal day and the day of death that creates the fear. The unknown here becomes the lack of knowledge about how long the deterioration will take – coupled with the degree to which one fights the deterioration. This is very much a personal decision – I have already expressed my views when considering cancer and its implications. I do believe that the actual patient, where capable, should be at the forefront of the decision-making as to the degree of medical interventions that should be endured. Here, we are perhaps returning to considerations of pain rather than fear – although the two are undoubtedly inexorably linked.

Perhaps one of the variables is each individual's belief of the concept of 'the afterlife', in its different concepts. Where the belief is of a total 'snuffing out' of the life-force – an ab-solute and total end to existence in any form – it can be very demoralizing (especially where your loved one has died be-fore you and you can feel no continuing connection). Where there is a belief in reincarnation and/or a continuity of the spirit, on the other hand, this can present encouragement through belief in the possibility of continuing links. These beliefs are very much down to each individual – and require a breadth of contemplation as well as study and discussion to allow a personal understanding of the process to develop.

The Bigger Picture

And so, we have pain, stress and fear – dealt with separately but undoubtedly very closely linked. By considering each objectively, with constructive awareness of past experiences and consideration of future potential strategies, we can pre-pare ourselves more positively for coping with the nettles singly and compositely, in each 'Now' moment that Life throws our way.

Bringing it Together

So, we've considered many situations and many strategies. They say that moving house, losing a job, divorce and the death of a close relative are the four most stressful things to cope with. My wife died after thirty-eight wonderful years together, so I've never experienced divorce; we had moved house eleven times during those years, gaining much enjoy-ment (although some frustration with solicitors and ven-dors along the way!), with any involved stresses outweighed by the new experiences gained. I have been 'allowed to go' more than once in my career path, although feeling pretty

mutual about the partings and hardly surprised! I have however experienced what I might consider to be more than my
fair share of direct involvement in death, as alluded to in
these chapters, and also including the discovery of a friend
who had committed suicide with a shotgun. The strategies I
describe have largely worked.

Rather than dwelling on any more personal experiences,
perhaps we could consider a hypothetical scenario, to cement some of the coping concepts together – and to review
ways of grasping and dealing with a collection of nettles.

Example: Struggling through a Bed of Nettles

Michael had been called into the boss's office that afternoon.
If he'd thought about it, perhaps he might have spotted the
signs – he'd only been with his present company for eight
or nine months and there had been rumours of a possible
takeover. He'd been too preoccupied with learning new systems and being out on the road to pay much attention to
developments.

The presence of the Human Resources Manager from
Head Office flagged up danger signs straight away. Behind
her back, she was called 'Doctor Death' by staff in the company – her presence invariably resulted in termination for
someone, with procedures followed to the letter.

And so it was that Michael found himself travelling home
on the bus (having had his company car keys tersely de-
manded at the point of being escorted from the premises).
The house was strangely silent when he closed the front
door quietly behind him. How was he going to break the
news to Sandra – they'd just paid the deposit for a Mediter-
ranean cruise that she'd been angling to go on for several

years – a bungalow for a week on the Isle of Wight was more his choice.

He picked up the note which was propped against the condiment set on the kitchen table. His eyes scanned through the writing, picking out salient words – 'fed up', 'boring', 'left you', 'John', 'met at the gym', 'Lyn picking up Sophie from school' and – there on the bottom 'Patch slipped her lead and was run over by a bus – her body's in the back garden for you to deal with – she was your dog after all'.

Michael slumped onto a chair with his head in his hands, sobbing uncontrollably. What was he to do?

Extreme? – absolutely! Possible? – maybe. Responses? – many and varied.

Let's consider the situations and possible strategies.

A Coping Strategy for Michael

We're looking at overall strategies only here. The details are in the previous chapters – or contact information is referred to within the text. The purpose of the exercise is more to consider the range of crisis problems in this case, establish sources and concerns Michael has to consider and prioritize – and give some consideration to his overlying coping strategies. You should also be able to embellish them or review alternative stances.

After a good cry to ease the initial overwhelming stress (if he can and if it helps – it does for most people), however long that takes, Michael should make himself a hot drink (not alcoholic) and sit down comfortably for a 'crisis meeting' with himself. A period of relaxed, focused breathing, coupled with a concentrated session on the 'fader technique' should help to get his mind more relaxed, able to think both logically and creatively. He should have paper and pen ready to make notes – this will help his thought-processes, his focus – and to cross-relate concerns and responses.

He remembers the equation:

CRISIS = SOURCE + CONCERNS.

What are the sources of his crisis? In no particular order for the moment, they are that:

- *He's lost his job*
- *His wife's left him*
- *He has potential financial problems ahead*
- *He is responsible for looking after his daughter Sophie*
- *His dog is dead in the back garden*

These are probably enough to be going on with for the moment! What would you say was Michael's first priority?

Yes – probably checking up on his daughter's whereabouts. A call to Lyn (the neighbour) should be first on the list. Depending on how friendly they are and how unselfish Lyn is, perhaps she would agree to look after Sophie until Michael gets his concerns sorted through to some extent.

The other sources probably group into job and finances; reaction to Sandra leaving and how to respond; longer-term care of Sophie and dealing with the dead body of Patch.

Allied with these external issues – and of extreme importance – is dealing with his own emotional fragility, caused by these various crises hitting him at the same time. He may be able to deal with this privately – but should be considering some level of support and assistance, whether it be at 'best friend' or professional level. Grief will return periodically, triggered by the various stresses which will be rising and falling – so our stress-management techniques in chapter three will be of ongoing value to Michael.

Let's take each of the sources of stress in turn, as presented above. These are not in any order of importance – so I'm not entering into any debate as to whether it's more important to rescue the marriage than it is to find another job, for example! We're only dealing at overview level here – I leave it to you, the reader, to consider the deeper detail, from the ideas presented in previous chapters.

Job and Finances

One of the benefits of the involvement of 'Doctor Death', the bizarre agent in HR, is that all the legal niceties will already have been completed. This should include financial settlements – but Michael may want to look into these to confirm that they are as expected. Union advice or the involvement of an employment lawyer might be considered. References should be arranged while matters are 'fresh' and any settlement package conditions agreed – including the situation regarding contact with previous clients, and so on.

Michael should look into his financial situation carefully, including the degree of continuing access which Sandra has to joint accounts – with reference to continuing mortgage and utility payments and the support of Sophie, for example. Depending on the state of his finances, the expected settlement and projected outgoings over the period prior to the possibility of finding renewed employment, Michael might be advised to discuss the situation with his bank, building society, and so on, sooner rather than later.

With regard to job prospects, Michael should contact any employment agencies he may be aware of – or has registered with in the past, to 'put himself back on the market' as soon as possible. This will probably also involve registering his CV on various websites as well. Depending on any conditions agreed and accepted with his previous employer, he may want to contact previous clients or companies, to discuss the possibility of employment on a permanent or even occasional consultancy basis. This is the time to call in favours, network and push his skills forward, while he is still fresh – and still potentially has remaining confidence – if he's coping with his concerns.

Marriage Situation

Responses here will depend on how the situation was between Michael and Sandra over the previous period of time. Nothing can really progress, one way or another, until contact is made between the two. The real depth of involvement between Sandra and the mysterious 'John from the gym' will also have a bearing on outcomes. Given the situation, Michael may or may not wish to pursue and plead with Sandra for a return to the status quo; Sandra may want to return ultimately, once the 'real' John has surfaced, perhaps! – or on condition that Michael's apparently boring level of *status quo* is improved!

Conversely, John might be Sandra's perfect man, in which case there will be little chance of reconciliation. One way or another, Michael needs to talk through his situation frankly with someone – either a close friend, relation or professional counsellor, to establish the next steps. Depending on outcomes, the longer-term care and custody of Sophie will have to be discussed as a priority.

Family Situation

Once Michael has his thoughts straightened out at an initial level, he needs to contact neighbour Lyn to discuss the situation. As he will presumably be at home for the initial few weeks, he should be able to care for Sophie – but there may be times when he needs to be away for job interviews (although so much of this tends to be conducted by telephone, Skype or internet application nowadays). Family, if living within easy access, might be asked to help, again depending on situations and relationships. Lyn might also agree to help, depending on the degree of friendship between her and Michael.

It would probably be expected that Michael should contact Sophie's school to update them with the situation, which could then set various official processes in motion. It is likely that Sandra's disappearance will have an adverse effect on Sophie – so Michael may experience increasing problems with dealing with his daughter. Once more, he should share his problems through discussion and seek any help he can access.

There is the possibility that Sandra may wish to have custody of Sophie – which would bring in a completely different level of negotiation, involvement of officialdom – and probably hard feelings.

Dealing with Patch

Although this is possibly the easiest nettle to deal with physically, it could be a difficult one emotionally (both directly and because it could become a focus of grief and frustration brought in from the surrounding situation).

Michael could consider burying Patch in the back garden (farmers can no longer bury dead livestock on their land, but the law is different in a domestic situation). Otherwise, he could arrange through his local vets' practice to have the body cremated, with the ashes returned for whatever rest-ing place he and Sophie decide. Any remaining grief will be gradually dealt with through quiet walks round previous haunts, as well as through open discussion of feelings. The death of a loved pet may not be on a par with human death – but should not be underestimated.

This review has only scratched the surface of Michael's overall crisis situation but hopefully serves to underline how the source – or sources in this case – can be quietly reviewed and acted upon. Although we have entered the technical level of response to many of the issues, many of the strategies applied are based on those described in chapter three. I suggest that you scan through this chapter again, to remind yourself about the range and their applications here. The benefits of focusing inwardly on the Now will assist both in considering each issue rationally and, at a deeper level, reaching a clearer awareness of inner beliefs.

In each real situation, the concerns and responses will of course differ, depending on all manner of issues which will be unique to that combination of events – but the overall coping processes applied will be similar.

'Freeing the Champion Within'

There is a full-length eBook with this title available for download on my website, which charts the fall and rise of the 'hero' Harry – whose initial situation is very similar to that of Michael's. Being a full-length book, it goes into a lot more detail about coping and responses, much of which is based upon Harry's spiritual awakening and his attempts at integrating new concepts into his new work situation.

If you're interested in reading this further illustrative example, check at the end of the 'Books' section in my website www.the-integrated-triangle.com.

Meditative Thought

Remaining for the moment on the subject of death, the following poem considers the possibility of reincarnation and the ways that elements of the continuity of the soul might function. It is included in the positive hope that it might bring encouragement to some who are troubled by the fear of dying. It's certainly worth a little contemplation.

Soul Passage

How do I go up to Heaven,
When the moment arrives to go?
Do I rise up in white clouds of glory
As a ghost, like the films all show?

What happens to me when I die, Sir?
Do I switch like a halogen light?
Or is there some energy left there
Continuing to shine out so bright?

Have you never heard of your soul, dear,
Or the links that we have throughout time?
The piece that comes down to sort karma
While our major soul stays up in line....

In the Light there, which many call Heaven,
Enjoying a blissful, full life
With other old souls we've encountered:
Relations, the buddy, the wife.

Our main soul can happily stay there
Enjoying the bliss that we bring

Until once again, karma will tell it
To return to resolve one more thing.

So the soul part will choose a new body
And downwards that soul spark will fly -
One more step on the path to enlightenment
As new incarnation – to try

To resolve karmic problems outstanding
And work for solution of this:
Then once more, as a spark, we can journey
From that body, to return to Bliss.

So think of your soul and your karma;
Think reincarnation and love.
Think of energy sparks and soul passage
They give purpose to life's every move.

We aren't just merely a body
That lives for a while and then dies,
But an ongoing soul powered by karma
To resolve, then return to the skies.

We all are involved in this progress
At varying speeds, to be sure
We're all those bright glimmers of love-light,
Emanations from source, oh so pure!

So link hands and pray with your neighbour
Feel energy passing on through.
We all are God's soul lights in action
If you can but believe it's all true.

Chris Sangster

CHAPTER TEN

DRIVING YOUR LIFE FORWARD

Personal Empowerment and Holistic Tenets

FOCUS ONCE more on the energy of love and light. I have tried to establish in the preceding chapters that there is an all-pervading Energy – you may call it 'the Universe', 'the Oneness', 'Nature', or 'God' – that makes all things possible. Possible, I stress – not perfect. We have seen, through the duality of light and dark, positive and negative and all the other apparent opposites, that in reality the negative will ground the positive and darkness emphasize the light. The balance is necessary. We also saw, through our images of the pendulum, that balance takes some time to achieve! In global terms, the light is the energy-giver, directly through sunlight and indirectly through the stimulation of chlorophyll to enrich the food which is so necessary to keep us alive. In personal terms, this positive light is what we are working at developing within ourselves. External emanations are greater in some than others, to be sure – but internally, the 'seeds' are there germinating in all.

This 'light-germination', in the form of personal empowerment, will be the focus in this chapter. In terms of personal development, we've given much of our concentration in the book so far to considering coping strategies and the situations where these can be applied. Additionally, we've been reviewing 'good practice' activities which we can use, to reduce the need for coping strategies in the first place. Notice – that's personal development rather than personal empowerment.

What is Empowerment?

So, what is empowerment and why the difference? The dictionary definition of empowerment is 'giving the power to enable someone to do'. Whereas development is giving someone the skills potentially to do something, empowerment involves the additional 'secret ingredient' which enables them to do it.

We can, of course, empower ourselves, with a little initial effort involved in identifying the skills. In the spiritual sense (which we've never been far away from in these chapters), there is that additional, inspirational element. Inspiration – the breathing in of the light.

Light, Energy, Vibration

We're probably all aware of the concept of atoms and molecules vibrating. These are nature's building blocks – vibration is everywhere! Radio waves penetrate a 'solid' stone wall because the atoms in the stone are vibrating, creating momentary 'spaces' for the waves to pass through. And, through this vibration, even stone emanates an energy. In our conservatory, I have a large bowl which contains hundreds of small stones – each individually picked up from every sacred place worldwide I have visited, or meditated at or whose energy I have otherwise experienced.

My son Ross, bless him, also brought back many stones

from around the world while travelling, representing many of the sacred locations he and his wife visited. These are also in the bowl. Dowsing each individual stone with a pendulum indicates its energy; dowsing above the bowl in various positions shows a myriad of composite energies circling to left, right and all points in between. Energies are all around us – and in these years around 2012, are building and changing dramatically.

Like the stones, we emanate energy, although to a higher degree. We are empowered … or at least the potential energy is there. Like an electrical cell, we have the positive energy and, through focusing on being earthed, are ready to give forth that energy – that power.

We speak about someone being 'earthed' or 'grounded' when they can cope confidently with situations or where they view life quietly and with awareness. We can individually emanate that power and equally can receive that power from others – other people, other things, other locations, other thoughts and beliefs.

Example: Receiving the Power

As I have explained earlier, I was conscious of having my spiritual energy activated while living in Wiltshire, through initially meeting Yeva. She was a wonderful old(ish!) lady, who appeared to know virtually everyone who was anyone in the 'spiritual world'. She came to live in a cottage we owned and I spent many a happy hour talking with her – and the many fascinating people who came to visit. She encouraged and enlightened me in so many different ways – as well as introducing Gillean and me to Isabelle, an equally-wonderful sensitive with whom I still work.

Gil and I had moved to the Manningford area, relatively close to Avebury, without totally knowing why but, through the various people we met, it became apparent it was an important activation point for our empowerment and enlightenment. It is relatively easy to become absorbed in the aura of enlightenment in this area – there are so many sacred sites, circles, tumuli and long barrows around to visit and tune into. And so it was, linking in with Isabelle's group who are charged with healing and conducting the earth energies for the area (among a range of other positive activities).

Progressing further, Gil and I then moved to the relatively remote west coast of Scotland. Initially, we felt unsettled because the physical sacred sites were both fewer and much more widely scattered around the mainland and islands. Gradually, I found myself tuning into nature. We were blessed in living in an absolutely stunning location, overlooking Loch Garry, with woods, moors, water and fields all around us. The wildlife and my flock of sheep took my attention and taught me so much about life, co-existence – and the harsh realities of life and death. In working with this and the local community, both my empowerment and enlightenment grew dramatically, with many meaningful experiences and activities. It also reinforced the point that my earlier close love of nature as a child and teenager, living in the Spey valley in Scotland, had a part to play in building the foundations, although these had gone through a semi-dormant phase during my mid-years while I was earning a living in the cities of Glasgow, Portsmouth, London and Brussels.

And finally, with our move to central Hampshire (again, without any apparent reason for choosing a particular location), I find myself living in a geographic area which is charged with a rich variety of spiritual organizations, from the White Eagle Lodge to Chithurst Buddhist Monastery; from a disproportionate number of cathedrals to the Hamblin Trust, at Bosham House. There are other centres, too many to mention, all radiating forms of spiritual energy into the atmosphere we live in. Exposure to these and a vast range of erudite talks and workshops (encouraged by my enthusiastic partner Jackie, who 'sings very much from the same hymn sheet'!) has brought our mutual enlightenment path to a new level once more. It's a level that brings the realization that, although it can be clothed in a wide variety of outer display, there is really only one unified Wisdom, one Truth, providing a track that we must all progress along in our individual ways.

Key Wisdom

As well as the overwhelming impact of love, we have the simplicity of being. This simplicity helps us to feel grounded, safe and uncomplicated, manifesting our progressive attempts at achieving levels of selflessness and altruism (which we have been referring to consistently throughout). Applying the concepts behind simplicity of being, we can formulate the basic tenets of a spiritual way of life, as are set down later in this chapter.

In the previous chapters, I have established the importance of openly and co-operatively existing together in a stable work–life balance – sharing views, standards and experiences as kindred spirits, progressing gradually towards enlightenment. This progression can be slow and varied, as we search for the Truth. In the visualization in chapter five, we imagined our various paths intertwined along the track as we potentially influenced, assisted and (on occasion) impeded each other. In the reality behind this visualization however, each of us will similarly continue to progress apace, following our own selected sequence of goal milestones.

As well as discovering new ideas and concepts, hold onto the image of having a unique reservoir of knowledge that is internal to you – to each one of us – which allows us to have vision through intuition. Feel confident that your thoughts are inspired – if you can but progress in the assurance of knowing that your intuitive thoughts are true. Each one of us functions through this form of spiritual guidance.

Through this direction, the messages we all receive (and may give) are multi-levelled. The important truth will often stand behind the immediate meaning, encouraging us to think more deeply about our communications. Because the hidden significance often needs consideration and even lateral thinking before becoming apparent, we should dedicate the time to ponder these inner truths. Listen with the heart rather than the mind and those truths will become apparent.

Meditate for a while on the multi-level concept of 'embracing the nettles of life', for example!

Applying the simple but all-encompassing action of love in its totality (applying the wealth of meanings we have considered in preceding chapters), you should be capable of tapping into an immense reservoir of wisdom, through experience, awareness, reading, communication and the many other ways of progressing our state of enlightenment. As I quoted earlier, 'Life is a learning experience' – we are all constantly learning, if we maintain an open heart.

The final wisdom, which gives us a criterion and basis for all right thinking, is the ongoing effort to cement peaceful thought. Peace at individual, community, national and universal levels is an overall goal which is far from being achieved but is the focus of many groups and activities. And, standing the concept on its head, we also have peaceful means creating thoughtful action – as was practised by Gandhi, for example, or through the non-reactive stances taken by the Dalai Lama.

Pondering on these gives us a breadth of understanding and appreciation which allows us to view coping with life in all its various facets with hope and equanimity.

Developing the Skills

So, let's consider some of the criteria which you may find applicable towards developing your personal empowerment. You may find it useful to make some specific notes, to commit to particular responses for some of the issues. Occasionally, discussion areas may relate to previous responses so, if you haven't already noted what these were, your path might begin to meander somewhat!

Also, I'm not aware of the point along the track that you, dear reader, have reached, so please adapt this list to your own level of needs.

Exercise – Establishing some Foundations for Personal Empowerment

Try to respond to the following.

- Name one skill or capability you would like to develop further
- Considering this, how could you apply it positively?
- What support would you require, in order to develop and apply it?

- *What would your first priority be, to get it started?*
- *How would you check periodically, to ensure it's developing as intended?*
- *State, as specifically as you can, what you see your key goal to be*
- *What are your priorities, so that you can build your confidence?*
- *Considering the energies which drive you on, how do you identify these?*
- *Is there a different/supplementary direction in which you could aim your energy growth?*
- *Review where your empowerment stands at this moment. What's the next step?*

Carry out the same process for another skill or capability. Remember to make notes.

Moving Towards your Goal

I raised the point earlier that a good business manager is one who prepares the foundations to allow his or her staff to work and progress without blockages, discouragement and delays. That's empowering people – setting up the conditions, in order that the staff (or people generally) can action things confidently to achieve the kind of standards which have been set. This ability to meet standards – to cope with given criteria – works in business: it can work equally in life generally. Also, as implied very strongly in the exercise you've just completed above, you can easily empower yourself, if you think consistently and confidently along the correct lines.

As set out in the applications of the Wisdom slightly earlier, learn to believe in your own intuition. You might speak about that 'small internal voice' you hear sometimes, giving direction. You may think you're imagining it. Believe in it; listen to it; trust it; consider and act upon it – it often knows best, whatever you perceive it to be!

Remember those Plan As and Bs that the 'small internal voice' has helped you establish. If you decide initially on Strategy or Plan A, stick with it and work through the questions you've been considering recently. Stand by your intuition and the strength of your own convictions. Drive the ideas forward and you'll feel empowered – capable – confident that you can succeed.

But, if you really impact on that (apparently solid) brick wall … you may already have established a Plan B which will also have things going for it. Shelve A and focus on B, then get into the same process, with the same sense of conviction. Life is a learning experience, remember!

Getting There

We've all seen the graphical representation of that 'eureka moment' – the picture of the head, with a light bulb shining in a thought-bubble above it. That's the popular depiction of seeing the light. However, enlightenment doesn't come in a single flash! That's inspiration. The path to personal enlightenment is long – but far from weary! In ultimately reaching that final goal, teachers tell us that it takes eons of time (in terms of incarnations), with karmic progress our ongoing focus.

In more general terms, and borrowing some metaphors, many of us continue to seek the holy grail and/or await the second coming. Don't think of these as physical chalice or charismatic leader. What we seek is internal, not external, and our personal journey towards enlightenment is our path towards becoming more aware of what these externalized foci actually represent. Although it's easier for films and books to depict the chalice, treasure chest or ark of the covenant physically, it's the belief systems, the criteria and the spiritual way forward which we should be concerning ourselves with. In terms of channelled information, The Tibetan says:

> These intriguing pieces of information, which I at times convey, and which some of the students seem to regard as of vital importance, are of far less importance than the injunction to live kindly, speak words of gentleness and of wisdom, and practice self-forgetfulness.

White Eagle's take on the same subject is:

> Once you desire wisdom, not for your own satisfaction, not because of curiosity, but that you may labour to serve the whole earth, then your feet are placed in the path which leads ultimately to the house of light.

Altruism

Periodically in the book, I have mentioned 'altruism' and 'selflessness', encapsulated in the saying 'do as you would be done by'. Applying these, look upon enlightenment as a personal inner challenge towards living a better, more thoughtful and considerate life, rather than through applying external trappings or images. It's simple and straightforward, really. 'Serving the whole earth' sounds a lot to ask but the emphasis is on the serving rather than the earth. And how do we serve? By thinking of others; by acting in an unselfish way and by responding to needs and crises by first saying 'yes' and then figuring out how it can be done. Helping one person through their immediate (or longer term) problem is serving. It may not seem a lot, in the universal nature of things but service it certainly is.

You might have come across Conrad Lorenz's Chaos Butterfly Effect theory – 'the flutter of a butterfly's wings can cause a hurricane on the other side of the world'. In more realistic terms, you may recall, several years ago, the television pictures showing us the effect of those tsunami waves, generated off Sumatra, when they hit the coast of Sri Lanka, on the opposite side of the Indian Ocean (a distance considerably further than the length of the British Isles). Jackie and I experienced the effects of this in Sri Lanka, particularly in Galle, a fortified town on the southern tip of the island. Initially, the walls had protected the town from the surging waves but, once they were breached, there was an enclosed cauldron effect, with flood-level marks still visible on the walls around five metres above street level. That's the effect of transmitted energy. When we were there, we met a retired engineer from Sweden who was devoting his time to helping with the rebuilding work further north in the island. That's selfless service, at a more highly dedicated level than many currently achieve. However large, frequent or effective, it's all service and it all matters.

Exercise: Steps towards Enlightenment

Consider the following, presented in no particular order of degree or complexity. I suggest you note down your ideas as you progress, to help crystallize your thoughts.

- Picture/describe a detailed image representing the wonders of nature for you
- Recall an act of selflessness which you have carried out recently
- How is the concept of creative force/energy represented in your mind?
- If you can experience energy, describe how this manifests itself to you
- How would you describe/define altruism?
- Recall/describe a highly spiritual experience you have encountered
- Describe what you would consider to be a key universal Wisdom criterion
- Describe an image you have visualized while in a meditative state
- Describe a special bond/spiritual link you may feel with some other people
- Describe a karmic challenge you believe you are working through now

Although there is no progressive sequence implied in these steps and considerations, I would consider them all to be potential points of focus. You may not be able to respond immediately to some of them but give each some intense thought – really try to get into a 'Now' moment of inner thought. The information is likely to be 'in there', at a deeper level, waiting to be retrieved! If it doesn't manifest on this occasion, then it's an area you may bear in mind for future consideration and development.

Easing a Crisis

Enlightenment incorporates service – and service to others (or another) can assist with helping ease that person's crisis, at the same time as potentially developing your own stature. In more formalized vocabularies of enlightened development, we come across the concept of initiation. Some of us will have rather stereotypical visions of this, perhaps coloured by our ideas of how the Masons operate. However, we should think of initiation as a gradual expansion of consciousness through experiential stages, rather than some series of tests or ceremonies. The White Eagle Publishing Trust has a very good set of four books on Spiritual Unfoldment and another on Intuition and Initiation for those who feel ready to study this development area in greater depth.

Personal Example: Help from the 'Hierarchy'

We've been referring to White Eagle, The Tibetan and alluding to channelling in these latter chapters. Although I appreciate that these are concepts some readers will find difficult or impossible to deal with at this point, a developing awareness of them has certainly helped me immensely in my quest for further enlightenment. Therefore, can I ask you to just go with the flow of your intuition for a moment here!

In the channelling group I attend in support, Isabelle primarily channels Magi (or Merlin) – as I said previously, our group is charged with spiritually maintaining balance in the landscape around Avebury, Wiltshire. For me – and many others, channelling is a wonderful experience, where the channel or medium is bringing through the information from the Hierarchy (called the Inner Brotherhood by some). These are seen by us as Masters or enlightened beings who have reached that karmic point where further reincarnation is not required. (This, I might add, is straightforward verbal communication – no knocking on table-tops is involved!)

The wonderful thing that we experience, when we're asking specific questions, is that different beings can 'come through' to give teaching. It feels a bit like a Universal board meeting, with these various enlightened Masters not so much seated round a large table as being on call to be brought in as required, from wherever they are. It's a strange and wonderful experience – which I believe with Isabelle's channelling to be totally genuine – but I can understand if particular readers may have extreme doubts. Although I personally accept its authenticity, I also accept that (as with anything) there are inferior channels and fakes around to confuse general belief systems!

Involvement has certainly helped me to have the confidence to go with my intuition and hold firmly to what may be considered to be 'the strength of my own convictions' – but those convictions in truth probably incorporate much input from others!

So, from this point of belief, I can accept and believe that there is a 'team' of enlightened Masters, backed up by a further hierarchy of spirit guides, archangels and angels, who oversee our activities, in an energetic sense.

Returning to our intuition, we could thus consider that, when we have a sudden flash of inspiration – or reach a point of clear decision, we may be receiving insight from additional sources – what we summarize as that 'small internal voice'. If we have faith, we should grasp these ideas and work with them. Be inspired – feel convinced. Often, your immediate thought on a subject will be the correct one. Truth and wisdom are there, both internally and externally and we are constantly absorbing and processing these energies, if we grasp the opportunity and function through an open heart.

These inspired thoughts will certainly help us to formulate valuable coping strategies.

Spiritual Tenets

I wrote earlier about 'Spirituality in the Workplace' retreats, where Jeremy and I were trying to juxtaposition the worlds of spiritual or enlightened thinking with those of more work-a-day life. In some business contexts, I have in the past preferred to refer to these tenets as 'holistic', where the overall effect has an additional, beneficial impact, as this is often easier for some people to accept. The twenty 'holistic tenets' appear somewhere in every one of the books I have written, from 2000 onwards.

With the progress which we have all, I hope, achieved throughout this book, I think we can confidently now acknowledge the pure spirituality involved in the detail! The business world is more aware of the concept of 'synergy', which is basically the same, when applied to groups of people or activities. We get synergy in a team of people when their interactions create an output and effect which is more than would be expected from the same number of individuals.

And so, I bring you what I consider to be the twenty tenets for a more spiritual way of life. As before, there is no implied sequence or progression in the twenty statements but each one requires a degree of thought. Having presented the tenets as a continuous sequence, for ongoing reference purposes, I'll elaborate on some of them, for clarity's sake.

Twenty Tenets for a More Spiritual Way of Life

1. *build positive thought*
2. *be aware of yourself and how you affect others*
3. *believe in yourself and others*

4.   act as selflessly as you can
5.   allow time to do things properly
6.   give matters time to evolve
7.   allow yourself 'time out' for thinking
8.   rest, relax and practise meditation
9.   use visualization to concentrate thought
10. observe and learn from world affairs and history
11. work towards co-operation and away from egocentricity
12. consider the effects of your actions
13. apply spiritually-based judgments when seen as appropriate
14. do what ultimately feels right
15. reduce your dependence on stimulants and medication
16. believe in the healing power of positive thought
17. exercise in as natural an environment as possible
18. retain an overview of the bigger picture
19. maintain a focused view on your enlightenment path
20. amend your plans flexibly to maintain progress

Elaboration

Positive thought (1) is getting away from the 'yes … but' response. Much earlier in the book, I remarked on the preponderance of people identifying the negative rather than the positive aspects of an experience. It could be because it makes a better story – it might be because of the way the press and broadcasting media bombard us with bad news as being the only noteworthy news. Life is not all good news – that's for sure – but thinking positively, seeing the best in people and acknowledging what is good in life, all helps us see life in daylight, rather than overshadowed with darkness.

We have considered (2–4) the benefits of self-awareness

and belief and have also touched on the concept of selfless-ness. As we established earlier, an unselfish act will help others, while still having some positive impact on yourself. A selfless act often goes further, where you might step aside to allow someone else to act, foregoing the opportunity yourself. There are of course occasions for both.

When working as a team member (4), you can often allow others to flourish rather than always pushing yourself forward assertively. Thinking selflessly involves showing consideration to others and thinking how they – and you – fit into the 'bigger picture' mentioned later in the list. Then you will see reasons why you might be best at doing certain things, while others should come first when volunteering for alternative tasks. And that's not just because you don't fancy doing them! It's because the overall, holistic effect will be better, with everyone's skills being applied for optimum results.

The next four tenets (5–8) all relate to the best use of time. Don't rush into doing things. There's a learning style known as being an Activist (alternative styles are referred to as Theorist, Pragmatist and Reflector, which all tend towards functioning more slowly and contemplatively). Activists tend to function by trial and error, leaping enthusiastically into new experiences but often losing interest fairly rapidly. Developing oneself spiritually takes time and patience, as well as requiring consolidation times to see and apply new thinking within context. So act more pragmatically or reflectively (theorists are sometimes rather slow at getting round to action at all!)

These activities may be when we're considering our Plan A/B situations to establish the best way forward (8–9). Consider giving yourself thinking time and also rest and relaxation time where you can switch off. You may like to try meditating regularly – however, remember that with meditation it takes lots and lots of practice, in conducive conditions, to allow you to reach a truly altered state. It's a study in its own right – there are many courses and groups around which you may like to attend, if you start searching. Getting the right atmosphere is crucially important, to allow you to concentrate and enter the state. Remember the possibilities of achieving a deeper mindful 'Now' state.

So much (10) can be learned from history and world affairs. It seems sensible to consider these past experiences – not in the sense of 'it can't be done because we tried before and failed' but more 'when it was tried before, such and such was a key problem so, perhaps we should think through alternative strategies'. If the bell curve I mentioned earlier rose and fell in a certain way for a previous situation, perhaps we can learn from this when we try to maintain levels differently at the potential decay stage, next time round. 'History', as the saying goes, 'repeats itself' – but it doesn't have to. How often have we heard the phrase 'lessons will be learned' in situations where similar circumstances have happened previously? Consider past events and outcomes – and adapt from them.

I think we have now covered most of the other areas included in the list, so you should manage to elaborate further yourself. If not, discuss it with someone else. I would recommend that you return to these twenty tenets periodically, perhaps meditating on one you have selected as being relevant for that particular moment. You have the awareness and wisdom already – it merely requires focused thought and uninterrupted concentration to prepare the way for a range of coping strategies.

Now – Charting a Positive Way Forward

We haven't had the need specifically to consider developing coping strategies for the subject matter covered in this chapter. With regard to focusing on the Now, when considering our gradual empowerment or enlightenment, there will be steps and stages along the path when this will be brought to the fore – where we are totally present in that moment and nothing else matters. This can be achieved during heightened moments of meditation and mindfulness – it is also an important element of the slide fader technique I have described periodically. Really focusing on the 'Now' moment goes beyond merely not thinking about past and future – it is a centred (almost blissful) state of mind when absolutely nothing external to the moment is considered at that instant. It is often described as 'going inward' – some consider it to also involve communication through the third eye area of the brow, by activation of the pineal and pituitary glands.

As we established in our exercise sections, your path of development will often involve considering particular examples, experiences or areas of awareness which will help you progress forward along your way. Any 'coping' involved in enlightenment should be very much of the interesting and positive kind! It may, on occasion be tinged with frustration, as things take longer than you would prefer, to grow and flourish. But your efforts, rather than being focused on finding ways of coping with the frustration, should instead be concentrating on seeking the way forward, through reading, conversation and reflection.

Remember the saying 'prevention is better than cure'. As we've progressed through these chapters, coping has subtly moved from being a way of handling stress, disappointment and frustration, to the more confident stance of deciding what are the best strategies to prepare the foundations properly for positive outcomes.

You have the skills and competency to move forward – the Wisdom is available, for you to find. Check on some of the books listed in the Resources section at the end – the information's there. Attend talks; visit libraries; join discussion groups – the sources await you! Also, you'll usually find many people around who will be pleased to help if you ask – it's that selflessness again. Go forward on your path!

Meditative Thought

I wrote the poem overleaf some time ago and long before I considered the content of this chapter – but it covers so much of what the chapter includes that it seemed a perfect summary!

Meditate on the Teachings

Hear the Wisdom, so clear and proclaiming,
Say – 'Receive just as well as you give,
See sense in the bigger picture –
Time to think, to seek, to live.

Do as you would be done by
Without ceremony, idol or rites,
The Wisdom as path to Enlightenment
It's a way of life so bright'.

The message gains many good teachers
To enlighten, empower and love,
The power's in the soul, not the body -
The energy comes from above.

The teaching is borne by soul passage;
Incarnations mean little at all,
Concentrate now on the Wisdom
Not the head-dress or ankh or orb/ball.

The Hierarchy – as spirit companions –
Support us and show us the way,
If only we ask and seek guidance
To help us progress, day to day.

Look to the teaching, not teacher
See the energy: truth in crown flame,

From the Indian, Buddha or angel,
The energy light's just the same.

Find the knowledge, respond to the reason,
See the truth as it links with today,
Think of involvement and action
Spirit guides show us the way.

Adapting, resolving, applying,
Take the wisdom and link it to light;
See the message, not dwell on the messenger
And that message shows Wisdom so bright.

The Hierarchy, as Brotherhood teachers
Show us ways that the Wisdom applies,
It's our task to think, seek and live it
As it all manifests through our eyes.

The message is – keep it all simple.
The teachings are there for your soul;
Wisdom schools are a method of focus:
Simple truths, not a form of control.

So disregard portraits and icons
Gain the soul light and message from high;
It's the way to absorb the great Wisdom -
Which is blissful to do, if you try.

                                        Chris Sangster

VARIED NETTLES: EVOLVING A SELF–HELP STRATEGY

AS A FINAL, interactive, review section, I'd like to highlight a few areas which will benefit from some deeper thought. I find that in reading any book (and mine is no exception), there's a lot of information that can just pass onwards without being consolidated, if I don't go through the process of reinforcing the thought-processes by doing exercises, giving it further applied thought or discussing the implications with others.

There's a mantra we used to recite when training Training Managers in learning techniques –

I hear and I forget; I see and I remember; I DO and I understand.

This is your opportunity to learn through doing!

You're going to need that notebook and pen again – and you may, on occasion, have to refer to your previous responses. (If you inadvertently forgot to respond earlier (!) you may have to spend a little time reading the previous exercises again and formulating some answers). This is your future we're considering, after all, so it's worth a bit of effort!

I'll be selecting particular areas involving coping which I consider will benefit from further thought. That doesn't of course mean that these are the only important considerations incorporated in the contents – do return to the chapters you feel are most relevant to you and delve ever deeper. Like the inspirational sayings I've included, each message often comes at several different levels of understanding, if you pause and think about it. Don't just settle for the first response – explore further!

I'll note the chapter that each 'review thought' comes from – so for example, the background detail for 'R3' will be found in chapter three. If you're interested, there's a more detailed review chapter download available in the Books section of my website, www.the-integrated-triangle.com.

———

Let's start with considering a personal crisis (which you were asked to think through in **CHAPTER ONE**).

R1. In that crisis, what would you consider to be the key source – and what were your main concerns (using the definitions given in chapter one)?

In the light of your reading now, what might you have done differently?

There are no 'answer sections' to these questions – and subsequent ones – in this review section. The detail is there in the text and I hope now instilled in your mind, if you've followed the content of the book. If not, check back with the relevant chapter again – or discuss the question with your mentor if you have one.

If you really get stuck, send a brief email to chris.sangster@ btinternet.com. I won't promise to give you an answer by return, but I'll certainly get back to you with a (brief) response to your questions or ideas, relative to the book's contents.

Further than that, it's up to you to establish your own coping strategies – becoming involved and thinking through strategies yourself is part of the solution!

In **CHAPTER TWO**, you could think of mindfulness as being totally focused and aware of the present moment – the Now - and the activities, experiences, thoughts and sensations which are going on around you at that instant. There is also a deeper 'Now' level, where the focus is more within – perhaps when in a Theta state of meditation.

R2. When involved in repetitive/boring tasks, how can you use mindfulness and focus on the Now to maintain interest, progress and standards?

(Bear in mind the envelope-stuffing example but think of a similar example that you may have been involved with).

Before we leave this review of the content of chapter two, focus on how thinking in the Now will help you cope more easily with your day-to-day life. Make some notes.

———————————

CHAPTER THREE considers a wide range of coping strategies – you should use it as the central reference point when thinking of responses to specific problem examples in the future. Extending 'Now' thinking, taking each day (and each section of the day) as it comes and focusing on progressing positively through it, is a good starting point.

R3. Spend a little time consciously breathing, as described in the chapter. Sit up straight-backed with hands on thighs or stand upright. Notice how you feel after doing this deeply for several minutes.

The chapter considers seven different strategies for coping with a range of problem areas that we might encounter. These problem areas included financial affairs, family, work, the death of a relative. Think of the theoretical case study involving Michael's traumas in chapter nine. You will undoubtedly be able to think of others, from your own life-experience. Spend some time considering the deeper implications.

Remember to consult this chapter in the future, when trying to apply coping strategies for the specific areas covered in later chapters.

CHAPTER FOUR looked at various aspects of and approaches to healing.

> **R4. If you're aware of anyone involved in spiritual healing, ask to talk to them about healing, to get a better insight into how it's seen to work.**

We considered the responsibilities and pressures which relations involved in caring experienced. As we established, caring happens at all levels, from fairly constant supervision to degrees of involvement in direct nursing of the patient/member of the family. Whatever the level, one of the major coping aspects is the unremitting constancy of the situation, which can lead to the carer feeling rather trapped and overwhelmed.

> **R4. If you are aware of anyone – member of family, friend, neighbour – who is involved in caring, talk to them about their experiences and any coping situations which they might find difficult. How could you help?**

Try to become more aware of – and even involved in – the overall healing process, from conventional medical interventions to spiritual healing involving absent and contact methods. Different forms work for different people – try to respond to their beliefs with a degree of selfless understanding. Your role is to support, not undermine!

In **CHAPTER FIVE**, we considered the broader interpretations of the concept of applied love – and how it manifests itself through more general emotions such as respect, understanding, involvement and intuition. By consciously applying these, we can build positive and co-operative relationships in our dealings with others.

> R5. Have you ever volunteered to do anything? Think of the relationships and activities you experienced – how did these affect other people?

> R5. In these kinds of situations, how would you describe the 'love feelings' that became part of the way you carried out the activities?

This chapter included considerations about positive and negative, in terms of light and darkness. It established that we required both (a duality) for balance – and that efforts to respond positively to the darker moments of our life would progress our positive thoughts more dynamically.

> R5. Considering Love as Light, have you experienced a situation where you have had to adjust your way of life in some way, to move from a dark phase towards something more light and positive?

The final section of the chapter was a visualization of progress of personal paths along the track. It involved considering not only how your individual path evolved – but also how this path might influence the paths of others (and vice versa).

> R5. Did you spend some time experiencing the visualization, either by getting someone to read it to you while you meditated, or by recording it to play back? If not, have a go at doing it now – it really is worthwhile!

CHAPTER SIX: using sound is a wonderful means of coping with stress, tiredness and concern. Some of us gain relaxation by listening to music, or going for a walk in the peaceful countryside (which still of course has its natural sounds). Others of us use instruments to play our own music – or create our own sounds. Sound is used in some healing techniques, either as background music or through the use of specific instruments (such as gongs, singing bowls, Freenotes or shamanic drums, for example).

R6. In recent years, have you ever sung or played music with others? If so, have you ever experienced the effects of entrainment (sounds merging together within the group)? If so, recall the experience in as much detail as you can – with special attention paid to the positive effects received by yourself and the others.

R6. If you have ever experienced chanting – either real or recorded – what would you say were the effects and benefits which you might gain from involvement?

Many stressful situations at work or in life generally are caused by poor communication – both spoken and written. **CHAPTER SEVEN** concerns itself as much with methods of communicating more effectively, to prevent misunderstanding – as it does with strategies for coping with the effects of poor communication, thereby reducing stress.

R7. Can you think of an example in the past months where you got into a relatively stressful argumentative situation? If yes and with reference to the various response options given early in the chapter, analyse how the situation progressed – and how it might have progressed differently, given changed responses and reactions.

> **R7.** *Have you ever given a relatively formal presentation to a group of people? If so, what do you find the hardest part of the overall activity – and how might you improve your technique, to make it easier for you to cope?*

Communication lies at the root of many problematical situations in life – often because the language, knowledge or awareness levels vary so much between the different people involved in the discussion. Maintaining an awareness of how your message is being received – and adjusting it accordingly where necessary – is one of the first steps towards effective communications.

In **CHAPTER EIGHT** we consider the various implications of work–life balance – and how we can use these in coping strategies. Prioritizing time is a key issue, although we initially focused on the more spiritually-based aspects of love, harmony and service.

> **R8.** *From your awareness of your work–life balance, what one particular element of your life would you say was most out of balance? From the approaches described in the chapter, how do you think you might 'rebalance' this element?*

> **R8.** *From the list of criteria that suggest common characteristics of a 'spiritual person', which one would you select as the most important area – the one you might want to work on first?*

In **CHAPTER NINE**, we consider the various conditions that potentially have 'knock-on' effects for us – and which we can find extreme difficulties in coping with. The chapter reviews a whole range of situations and considerations, with reference to the coping strategies discussed in chapter three. It also links with our earlier considerations of the effects of dwelling on the past or becoming concerned with possible future repercussions – and the benefits of thinking in the Now.

R9. In order to reduce your own stress levels (and reinforce the working standards you expect from others), consider how you would say 'no' positively but in a non-confronting way. Thinking of a real situation you might potentially experience (or have experienced), plan a strategy for reaching a compromise outcome.

R9. This chapter covered the concept of 'Type 'A' stress', listing a range of indicators that can be applied. Checking through the list again, are there any of the indicators which you'd honestly say applied to you, to some large extent?

In the final chapter **(CHAPTER TEN)**, we first considered empowerment and then reviewed how this would progress in greater detail towards enlightenment. We also reviewed light and energy and how these might be considered to be the 'lifeblood' of our existence.

R10. Thinking back through your life experiences to date, can you think of a specific activity or occasion where you felt particularly empowered – resulting in greater involvement, contentment and a better outcome? What was it?

R10. How would you describe experiencing a degree of enlightenment in your life? Can you think of any situation where you felt enlightened (or inspired) to any degree? Think about it – or make notes – to establish how you might proceed further with this experience.

R10. Considering the list of twenty tenets for a more spiritual way of life, select three or four you think you might benefit

from developing. Taking each in turn, review a few strategies
that you might apply to making this improvement – and set
yourself goals that you can progress towards.

The purpose of this Review Chapter has been to draw your attention to some of the key areas covered in the book – and stimulate you to think about them in greater detail. It has also been trying to encourage you to think about some of your own experiences – and how you might have applied strategies in a different, or more complex way, on occasion. A more detailed version is available in the book section of my website.

Many of these questions are open-ended. You may therefore find it useful to return to them periodically, to review your current stance and progress. Discuss your thoughts with your mentor, if you can find someone to help you. My email address is **chris.sangster@btinternet.com**. As I said previously, I can't promise to reply by return but I will get back to you with a brief response, if you have any questions you want to share.

Good luck in your quest towards enlightenment – and your efforts at coping more confidently with those various nettles of life. Embrace them confidently!

A Final Meditative Thought

I should like to end with a poem entitled 'The Energy of Alba' which I wrote concerning the energies of nature, energies that I experienced during my return to my native land for a period of seven years with Gillean – between our initiation in Wiltshire and my broadening of experience more recently with Jackie down in Hampshire. I feel these energies very close to my heart.

The Energy of Alba

My mind responds to silence vast
As cares and pressures distant fade;
Drifting thoughts to the soul abound;
Ears tune in to latent calm
As body rests in moss and heath –
The energies of life surround.

Wind in trees and wet on stone –
Distant cries declare domain
From stag, or hawk, or human call,
Sounding gently in the peace:
Unheard by those who do not feel
Or tune in to the sense at all.

Mountains fall down to the coast.
Tracts of land where no life shows
Meet our gaze with silent might –
Greens and purples, greys and browns;
Spumes of white caress the shore –
This palette vast: a wondrous sight.

Energies we may not see
But sensing all around we feel;
Magnetic pull without the coil,
Earth alive to those aware
Some as fairy, pulse or orb,
Respond as friend, react as foil.

Amidst the silence, sound reveals –
Subtle though each tone may be
Calling for attention rapt,
Tuning ear and focused mind;
Identify each act or call –
Earth energy or creature trapped.

Hear the power of aqueous flow
In waterfall or sea or stream.
Move relentless, night and day,
Timeless energies to yolk
With Man's requirements soundly met
Once fuel and wind have had their say.

Verdant greens of different tints
Illumined brightly all around
Display a heightened power to view,
Moss and branch and leaf and blade
Send their vibrant message out:
Enlightenment in every hue.

Scotland's majesty to prize
In hidden valley, lapping shore
Swirling mists as traveller climbs.
She is my homeland, deeply felt,
Bringing sense of thoughts profound
That soothe the heart, in pensive times.

                                        Chris Sangster

RECOMMENDED RESOURCES

As will have become apparent throughout the chapters, my earlier involvement in more conventional business training and development has been progressively coloured – and indeed overshadowed on occasions – by both spiritual and alternative therapeutic considerations and applications. In some situations, my resultant stance reflects a practically-based amalgam of some or all approaches, as I firmly believe in wisdom being at the realization end of the learning, application, realization continuum. The following book resources reflect this range of applications and interests.

STRESS MANAGEMENT

Coping with Stress at Work	Jacqueline M Atkinson	Thorsons
Living with Stress	Cooper, Cooper and Eaker	Penguin
Happiness and How it Happens	'The Happy Buddha'	Leaping Hare
You can Heal your Life	Louise L Hay	Eden Grove
Instant Calm	Paul Wilson	Penguin
Type 'A' Behaviour and your Heart	Friedman & Rosenman	Random House
Aromatherapy Stress Management	Christine Westwood	Amberwood
Pharmacy for the Soul	Osho	St Martin's Griffin
Discover Inner Peace	Mike George	Duncan Baird

RELATED SPIRITUAL DEVELOPMENT
1. Stages in enlightenment / coping with life

At www.whiteaglepublishing.org you will find the full range of White Eagle books. Especially recommended are:

Heal Thyself

A Little Book of Healing Comfort
A Guide for Living with Death and Dying
Spiritual Unfoldment 1 − 4
First Steps on a Spiritual Path
Further Steps on a Spiritual Path
White Eagle on Living in Harmony
White Eagle on The Great Spirit
White Eagle on The Intuition and Initiation
The Light Bringer
Treasures of The Master Within (short meaningful passages)
The Quiet Mind (short meaningful passages)
The Best of White Eagle (longer meaningful extracts from various books)

Also see:

The H.E.L.P. Book	Raja	Findhorn Press
The Silent Road	W Tudor Pole	Neville Spearman
A Vision of the Aquarian Age	Sir George Trevelyan	Coventure
The Prophet	Kahlil Gibran	Senate
Ancient Wisdom, Modern World	The Dalai Lama	Little, Brown & Co
The Gnostic Gospels	A Jacobs (editor)	Watkins

2. Spiritual Channellings

The Only Planet of Choice	P V Schlemmer	Gateway
Bringers of the Dawn	B Marciniak	Bear & Co
Alignment to Light	Julie Soskin	Ashgrove
Ponder on This (compilation)	Alice Bailey	Lucis Press
The Dawn of Change	Eileen Caddy	Findhorn Press

3. Mindfulness and its Applications

The Art of Mindful Walking	Adam Ford	Leaping Hare
Finding Happiness	Christopher Jamison	Weidenfeld
Parami − Ways to Cross Life's Floods	Ajahn Sucitto	Amaravati
The Power of Now	Eckhart Tolle	Hodder Mobius

The Meditation Lifestyle   Colum Hayward   Polair
SOULution – Holistic Manifesto William Bloom   Hay House
Downshifter's Guide to Relocation Chris & Gillean Sangster howtobooks
Messages/Echoes (2 book set)   Chris Sangster   direct from author

MANAGEMENT 'BEST PRACTICE'

Spirituality in the Workplace Marques et al   Personhood
Don't Sweat the Small Stuff   Richard Carlson   Hodder
Funky Business   Ridderstrale   Prentice Hall
Karaoke Capitalism   Ridderstrale   Prentice Hall
First, Break all the Rules   Buckingham   Pocket Books
Mindstore   Jack Black   Thorsons
The Dilbert Principle   Scott Adams   Boxtree
Coach Yourself   Grant & Greene   momentum
Coaching for Performance   John Whitmore   Nicholas Brierley
Growing Workplace Champions   Chris Sangster   Studymates
Brilliant Future   Chris Sangster   Prentice Hall
How to be a Better Manager   Armstrong   Kogan Page
The Empty Raincoat   Charles Handy   Arrow
Spectacular Teamwork   Blake, Mouton & Allen   Sidgwick & Jackson
Seven Secrets of Inspired Leaders Dourado & Blackburn Capstone
Creating Excellence   Hickman & Silva   Allen & Unwin
'A' Time   James Noon   V N R
The Frontiers of Management   Drucker   Guild Publishing
A Passion for Excellence   Tom Peters & N Austin   Guild Publishing

MUSIC THERAPY

Healing Power of the Human Voice James D'Angelo   Healing Arts Press
Sound Health   Steven Halpern   Harper & Row
Free your Voice   Silvia Nakkach   Sounds True
Harmonograph   Anthony Ashton   Wooden Books
Shifting Frequencies   Jonathan Goldmen   Light Technology

INDEX

POEMS